Playing wit
Presen
Rudyard Kipling's

The Jungle Book
FOR KIDS

(The melodramatic version!)

For 6-16+ actors, or kids of all ages
who want to "monkey" around!

Creatively modified by
Khara C. Barnhart and Brendan P. Kelso
Rudyard Kipling illustrated by Adam T. Watson
Cover layout illustrated by Shana Hallmeyer
Cover characters by Ron Leishman
Special Contributor: Asif Zamir

3 Melodramatic Modifications of Kipling's Novel
for 3 different group sizes:

6-8+ actors

9-12+ actors

13-16+ actors

Table Of Contents

For Bodhi
- KCB

Sincere gratitude for Ron Leishman,
Your art has inspired thousands
of kids to love the classics!
Thank you!
- BPK

Playing with Plays™ – Rudyard Kipling's Jungle Book for Kids

Copyright © 2004-2018 by Brendan P. Kelso, Playing with Plays LLC
Characters on the cover are ©Ron Leishman ToonClipart.com

For performance rights please see
page 6 of this book or contact:

contact@PlayingWithPlays.com

www.PlayingWithPlays.com

Printed in the United States of America
Published by Playing With Plays LLC

ISBN: 1517392462
ISBN: 978-1517392468

Foreword

When I was in high school there was something about Shakespeare that appealed to me. Not that I understood it mind you, but there were clear scenes and images that always stood out in my mind. Romeo & Juliet, "Romeo, Romeo; wherefore art thou Romeo?"; Julius Caesar, "Et tu Brute"; Macbeth, "Double, Double, toil and trouble"; Hamlet, "to be or not to be"; A Midsummer Night's Dream, all I remember about this was a wickedly cool fairy and something about a guy turning into a donkey that I thought was pretty funny. It was not until I started analyzing Shakespeare's plays as an actor that I realized one very important thing, I still didn't understand them. Seriously though, it's tough enough for adults, let alone kids. Then it hit me, why don't I make a version that kids could perform, but make it easy for them to understand with a splash of Shakespeare lingo mixed in? And voila! A melodramatic masterpiece was created! They are intended to be melodramatically fun!

THE PLAYS: There are 3 plays within this book, for three different group sizes. The reason: to allow educators or parents to get the story across to their children regardless of the size of their group. As you read through the plays, there are several lines that are highlighted. These are actual lines from the original book. I am a little more particular about the kids saying these lines verbatim. But the rest, well... have fun!

The entire purpose of this book is to instill the love of a classic story, as well as drama, into the kids.

And when you have children who have a passion for something, they will start to teach themselves, with or without school.

These plays are intended for pure fun. Please DO NOT have the kids learn these lines verbatim, that would be a complete waste of creativity. But do have them basically know their lines and improvise wherever they want as long as it pertains to telling the story. Because that is the goal of an actor: to tell the story. In A Midsummer Night's Dream, I once had a student playing Quince question me about one of her lines, "but in the actual story, didn't the Mechanicals state that 'they would hang us'?" I thought for a second and realized that she had read the story with her mom, and she was right. So I let her add the line she wanted and it added that much more fun, it made the play theirs. I have had kids throw water on the audience, run around the audience, sit in the audience, lose their pumpkin pants (size 30 around a size 15 doesn't work very well, but makes for some great humor!) and most importantly, die all over the stage. The kids love it.

One last note: if you want some educational resources, loved our plays, want to tell the world how much your kids loved performing Shakespeare, want to insult someone with our Shakespeare Insult Generator, or are just a fan of Shakespeare, then hop on our website and have fun:

PlayingWithPlays.com

With these notes, I'll see you on the stage, have fun, and break a leg!

SCHOOL, AFTERSCHOOL, and SUMMER classes

I've been teaching these plays as afterschool and summer programs for quite some time. Many people have asked what the program is, therefore, I have put together a basic formula so any teacher or parent can follow and have melodramatic success! As well, many teachers use my books in a variety of ways. You can view the formula and many more resources on my website at: PlayingWithPlays.com

- Brendan

OTHER PLAYS AND FULL LENGTH SCRIPTS

We have over 25 different titles, as well as a full-length play in 4-acts for theatre groups: Shakespeare's Hilarious Tragedies. You can see all of our other titles on our website here: PlayingWithPlays.com/books

As well, you can see a sneak peek at some of those titles at the back of this book.

And, if you ever have any questions, please don't hesitate to ask at: Contact@PlayingWithPlays.com

ROYALTIES

If you have any questions about royalties or performance licenses, here are the basic guidelines:

1) Please contact us! We always LOVE to hear about a school or group performing our books! We would also love to share photos and brag about your program as well! (with your permission, of course)

2) If you are a group and DO NOT charge your kids to be in this production, contact us about discounted copyright fees (one way or another, we will make this work for you!) You are NOT required to buy a book per kid (but, we will still send you some really cool Shakespeare tattoos for your kids!)

3) If you are a group and DO charge your kids to be in the production, (i.e. afterschool program, summer camp) we ask that you purchase a book per kid. Contact us as we will give you a bulk discount (10 books or more) and send some really cool press on Shakespeare tattoos!

4) If you are a group and DO NOT charge the audience to see the plays, please see our website FAQs to see if you are eligible to waive the performance royalties (most performances are eligible).

5) If you are a group and DO charge the audience to see the performance, please see our website FAQs for performance licensing fees (this includes performances for donations and competitions).

Any other questions or comments, please see our website or email us at:

contact@PlayingWithPlays.com

The 15-Minute or so
The Jungle Book for Kids

By Rudyard Kipling
Creatively modified by
Khara C. Barnhart and Brendan P. Kelso
6-8+ Actors

CAST OF CHARACTERS:

MOWGLI: random human boy living in the jungle

[1]**PARENT WOLF:** Mowgli's wolf parent

SHERE KHAN: tiger who wants to eat Mowgli for lunch!

BALOO: a bear who teaches Mowgli the Laws of the Jungle

BAGHEERA: a panther who looks out for Mowgli

[2]**KAA:** a hungry, old and powerful python

[2]**AKELA:** leader of the wolf pack

[1]**MESSUA:** Mowgli's adopted human mom

Any extras can be:

MONKEY-PEOPLE: vain, silly animals (all actors not onstage in a different role play MONKEY-PEOPLE)

WOLVES: If there are more than 7 actors, then extra actors can play wolves on stage and add lines as they want.

BUFFALO: the audience!

The same actors can play the following parts:

[1]PARENT WOLF and MESSUA

[2]KAA and AKELA

ACT 1 SCENE 1

(enter PARENT WOLF and BAGHEERA)

PARENT WOLF: Oh hi, Bagheera. What's happening in the life of a panther?

BAGHEERA: I wanted to warn you. Shere Khan's in town again.

PARENT WOLF: The tiger? What's he doing in this part of the jungle?

BAGHEERA: What tigers do. You know, hunt, eat, hunt again, eat... hunt....eat... *(trailing off)*

PARENT WOLF: *(play-acting like a tiger)* Oh look at me, I'm a mean ol' tiger, roar!!! *(there is a LOUD ROAR and GROWL from offstage, PARENT WOLF is a bit shocked)*

BAGHEERA: Listen! That's him now!

(enter MOWGLI, running off-balance, and falling down)

PARENT WOLF: Whoa! A man's cub! Look! *(ALL turn to look at MOWGLI)* How little and so... smelly, but cute! *(starts petting his hair)*

(BAGHEERA sneaks over to MOWGLI and whispers something in his ear. MOWGLI sighs and gets down on his knees to appear smaller; he remains on his knees throughout the rest of the scene and ACT1 SCENE 2)

MOWGLI: *(very sarcastically)* Gaa gaa. Goo goo.

(SHERE KHAN enters. PARENT WOLF hides MOWGLI behind her back)

SHERE KHAN: A man's cub went this way. Its parents have run off. Give it to me. I'll uh.... take care of him... *(as he rubs his belly)* you can TOTALLY trust me! *(gives the audience a big evil smile)*

PARENT WOLF: You are NOT the boss of us.

SHERE KHAN: Excuse me?! Do you know who I am? It is I, Shere Khan, who speaks! I'm kind of a big deal. And scary! GRRRRR.

PARENT WOLF: The man's cub is mine; he shall not be killed! So beat it; you don't scare us.

SHERE KHAN: Fine. But I'll get him some day, make no mistake! Muahahahahaha! ROAR! *(SHERE KHAN exits)*

PARENT WOLF: *(to MOWGLI)* Mowgli the Frog I will call thee. Lie still, little frog.

MOWGLI: *(to PARENT WOLF)* Frog?

PARENT WOLF: *(to MOWGLI and audience)* Yeah, I guess Rudyard Kipling liked frogs! But now we have to see what the wolf leader says.

(ALL stay on stage)

ACT 1 SCENE 2

(enter AKELA, BAGHEERA, and BALOO)

AKELA: Okay, wolves, let's get this meeting started! Howl!

WOLVES: Howl!! *(All WOLVES howl)*

PARENT WOLF: Akela, our great leader, I'd like to present the newest member of our pack, Mowgli the Frog!

AKELA: Hmmm, Frog, huh? If you say so.

(enter SHERE KHAN)

SHERE KHAN: ROAR! The cub is mine! Give him to me!

AKELA: Who speaks for this cub?

BALOO: *(speaking in a big, deep bear voice!)* I, Baloo the Bear, I speak for the man's cub. I myself will teach him the ways of the jungle.

BAGHEERA: I know I'm a panther, not a wolf, but if the pack takes him in, I'll provide you with a fat bull for your party. You guys like bull, right?

AKELA: Yeah! Cool, then it's settled. The panther, the bear, and us wolves will look out for the man-cub. *(high fives MOWGLI)* Guess that makes us man-cub's best friend!

MOWGLI: *(sarcastically)* Gaa gaa. Goo goo.

SHERE KHAN: Fine! *(begins to exit and mumbles to audience while shaking fist)* I would have gotten him too, if it weren't for those meddling jungle creatures! But I'll get him someday. Muahahahahaha! ROAR! *(exits)*

PARENT WOLF: Now, where were we?

AKELA: Oh, the man cub. He can join the pack. Take him away and train him as befits one of the Free People. Come on wolves; there's a fat bull calling our names!

(ALL exit howling)

ACT 1 SCENE 3

(enter BALOO and BAGHEERA)

BALOO: *(noticing BAGHEERA)* Checking up on me, eh?

BAGHEERA: Just want to make sure Mowgli's lessons are you know, actually happening. It has been some years since he came and joined the pack.

BALOO: I've been his teacher for all these years, and you still don't trust me? Fine. I've taught him how to tell a rotten branch from a sound one, how to speak politely to the wild bees, and the Stranger's Hunting Call. You know, the bare necessities!

BAGHEERA: Well, don't overdo it.

BALOO: Look, the jungle is a SUPER dangerous place. He needs to know all this stuff.

BAGHEERA: And remember, you're a bear, so be gentle with him!

BALOO: That's right, I AM a bear who TALKS. This story takes place in the JUNGLE. I am standing here talking to a PANTHER, and I spend my days teaching a HUMAN. If you hadn't noticed, none of this makes sense.

BAGHEERA: Huh... very true. Carry on.

(enter MOWGLI)

BALOO: Mowgli, show Bagheera what I've taught you. What do you say to the animal hunters in the jungle?

MOWGLI: *(loudly, with a low booming voice)* We be of one blood, ye and I.

BALOO: And to the birds?

MOWGLI: *(flaps arms like a bird)* Kaaaaaa! Kaaaaaaaaaa!

BALOO: And the Snake-People?

MOWGLI: *(wiggles on his belly)* Hissssssssssss Hissssssssssss *(darts tongue in and out of mouth)*

BAGHEERA: Amazing.

BALOO: Right? *(nodding head)*

MOWGLI: Yeah, and someday I shall have a tribe of my own, and lead them through the branches all day long!

BALOO: Wait, what? Tribe?

BAGHEERA: Branches?

BALOO and BAGHEERA: The Monkey-People!

MOWGLI: They're super cool! They said I was their blood brother, except that I had no tail, and should be their leader some day!

BAGHEERA: They have no leader. They lie. They have always lied. They will throw... stuff at you!

BALOO: Listen, man-cub. Those monkeys...they are outcasts. We do not drink where the monkeys drink; we do not go where the monkeys go; we do not hunt where they hunt...

MOWGLI: Come on, Baloo. *(mimics BALOO's voice and actions melodramatically)* We do not HUNT where they HUNT...

BAGHEERA: Dude, this is serious jungle stuff.

MOWGLI: Fine. No monkey business. *(chuckles to audience)*

BALOO: I think it's naptime.

BAGHEERA: Good idea.

(all three lie down onstage and fall asleep. Enter MONKEYS. They grab MOWGLI and run in a large circle and take him offstage while making lots of monkey noises. BALOO and BAGHEERA wake up to see the MONKEYS taking MOWGLI away)

MOWGLI: They've kidnapped me! Mark my trail! Help!

BALOO: Noooooooooooo! I can't believe I let them take him! Roll me into the hives of the wild bees that I may be stung to death, for I am the most miserable of bears! *(BALOO lies down on the floor and starts moaning and crying)*

BAGHEERA: Oh, get over yourself. This is NOT helping.

BALOO: *(stops crying)* I know, let's get Kaa!

BAGHEERA: The python?

BALOO: He is very old and very cunning. Above all, he is very hungry. Promise him many goats. No one can resist goats.

BAGHEERA: Goats? It's worth a shot, I guess. Let's go. *(BALOO and BAGHEERA begin walking around the stage; enter KAA)*

BALOO: There he is. *(to KAA)* Good hunting!

BAGHEERA: He's super old and can't hear well, remember?

BALOO: Oh right. Ahem. *(yells)* GOOOOOD HUUUUNTING, Kaa!! *(waves arms)*

KAA: I'm sssssuper hungry.

BAGHEERA: Of course you are, you old snake. *(KAA doesn't hear)*

BALOO: *(loudly and slow)* We are hunting...the MONKEY-PEOPLE.

KAA: What? Those chattering, foolish, vain, Monkey-People. I can't sssssssstand them.

BAGHEERA: *(loudly)* They have stolen away our man-cub.

KAA: Monkeyssss are thievessssss! Let'sss get them! Where'd they go?

BALOO and BAGHEERA: That way. *(they point in different directions)*

KAA: Brilliant. Well, let'sssssss try the monkey city.

BALOO: Ssssounds good.

BAGHEERA: We need to hurry...let's run! *(looks at KAA and yells)* Er, sssslither!

(ALL exit)

ACT 1 SCENE 4

(enter MOWGLI and MONKEYS. MONKEYS are having a party and making a mess; throwing bananas around, dancing and making lots of monkey noises. Every time MOWGLI tries to leave, a MONKEY pulls him back to center stage)

MONKEYS: *(chanting)* We are great! We are free! We are wonderful! We are the most wonderful people in all the jungle!

MOWGLI: You are full of yourselves.

MONKEYS: We all say so, so it must be true! Teach us how to make shelters from sticks and canes like men do!

MOWGLI: Um, I live with wolves, remember? In a cave! *(to audience)* These monkeys are crazy. *(MOWGLI sits center stage with the MONKEYS forming a circle around him. They tickle him, push him, and laugh at each other)*

(enter BAGHEERA, BALOO and KAA, tiptoeing up to the MONKEYS. They attack MONKEYS from all sides. MOWGLI is tugged between MONKEYS and BALOO. Finally KAA gives a very loud and fierce HISSSSSSSS, and the MONKEYS run offstage, scared)

BAGHEERA: Let us take the man-cub and go before they come back!

KAA: They won't come back. I'm pretty sssscary. Hissssssssssss......

BALOO: Wow, I am sore. *(to MOWGLI)* Art thou hurt?

MOWGLI: No. *(pause; makes fun of BALOO)* I art hungry!

KAA: A boy after my own heart!

MOWGLI: *(to KAA)* We be one blood, thou and I. Let'ssss go get some goatsssss!

KAA: Now you're talking! I love goatsssssss!

BALOO: *(to BAGHEERA)* Ssssee, I told you goatssssss would work.

(ALL exit)

ACT 2 SCENE 1

(enter BAGHEERA and MOWGLI)

BAGHEERA: Little Brother, how often have I told thee that Shere Khan is thy enemy?

MOWGLI: Not this again! I know, I know, he wants to kill me and eat me for lunch! But why? Why should any wish to kill me?

BAGHEERA: Because, Shere Khan is a hungry tiger! And 'cause you're a human. In case you forgot. Sort of a delicacy.

MOWGLI: Well, that's just not cool.

BAGHEERA: You know what you need for protection? The Red Flower! You should go and get some from the man village.

MOWGLI: How is a flower supposed to protect me?

BAGHEERA: It's not really a flower. That's just what we call it. It's FIRE!

MOWGLI: Well that makes more sense. I'll go get some. *(MOWGLI runs offstage and immediately returns holding a pot)*

MOWGLI: Got the fire...er, I mean, flower! *(winks to audience)*

BAGHEERA: Just in time...

(MOWGLI and BAGHEERA stay on stage)

(enter AKELA, SHERE KHAN, PARENT WOLF, and WOLVES)

SHERE KHAN: Akela, your time as leader of the wolves is over.

PARENT WOLF: Akela has been an awesome leader, Shere Khan.

SHERE KHAN: Bah! What do we have to do with this toothless fool! He is doomed to die!

AKELA: Hey man, not cool! I'm not toothless.

SHERE KHAN: It is the man-cub who has lived too long. Free People, he was my meat from the first. Give him to me!

AKELA: The rest of the pack wants to give him to the tiger. But, I said no! He is our brother in all but blood, and ye would kill him here! They are all cowards! They are afraid of you because, as they say it, "He is a man"!

BAGHEERA: *(to MOWGLI)* I think now's the time...

MOWGLI: You keep saying that "I am a man", so I guess instead of brothers, I need to call you dogs. And guess what? Dogs are scared of fire, aren't they? *(MOWGLI runs around to the WOLVES and SHERE KHAN and shakes the pot of fire in their faces. They all fling themselves to the ground in terror)*

SHERE KHAN: It burns! Oh how it burns!!

MOWGLI: Serves you right! Now I will go to men. I'm done with the jungle. *(walks over to PARENT WOLF)* Ye will not forget me?

PARENT WOLF: Never! Come soon! We be old and I loved thee more than ever I loved my cubs.

MOWGLI: I'll come back once I've killed Shere Khan. Do not forget me! Tell them in the jungle never to forget me!

SHERE KHAN: *(to self)* I won't forget you Mowgli! *(does an evil, evil laugh!)* Muahahahahaha! ROAR!

(ALL exit)

(enter MOWGLI and MESSUA from opposite sides)

MOWGLI: *(pointing at audience)* Look, humans! *(calls out)* We be of one blood, ye and I! *(to audience)* Oh wait, you probably don't speak jungle, do you?

MESSUA: *(to audience)* Look, a random wild boy! He looks like my son who was taken by the tiger a long time ago! What was his name??? Oh yeah, *(calls out to MOWGLI)* Nathoo! Nathoo!

MOWGLI: Bless you. By the way. I'm Mowgli.

MESSUA: Great! How did you learn how to speak?

MOWGLI: From a bear and a panther.

MESSUA: Oh...that's strange. Anyway, you're going to be my replacement son! *(she hugs him)*

MOWGLI: Hmmm, a bit weird, but, okay!

(enter BAGHEERA)

BAGHEERA: Psssssst! Hey, Mowgli!

MOWGLI: *(to MESSUA)* I'll be right back. *(runs to BAGHEERA)* Hey Bagheera, what's up?

BAGHEERA: Just wanted to let you know that, *(sniffs and plugs nose)* phew, you smell gross! Where was I... oh yeah, Shere Khan still wants to kill you.

MOWGLI: Thanks for the warning. Let me know when he gets close. *(runs back to MESSUA; BAGHEERA exits)*

MESSUA: Okay, look. Everyone has a job here, even the kids. You can go watch the buffalo graze in the field. *(points at the audience implying they are the buffalo)* Cool?

MOWGLI: Cool.

MESSUA: Be safe, Nathoo...Mowgli...whatever your name is. Bye! *(MESSUA exits; MOWGLI sits down)*

MOWGLI: Watching buffalo is booooring.

(enter BAGHEERA AND AKELA)

BAGHEERA: Shere Khan is back, Mowgli! He's waiting for you in the ravine!

MOWGLI: *(jumps up)* Awesome. I am not afraid of Shere Khan. We have big work in hand. I have an idea, see all these buffalo? *(he gestures to the audience)*

AKELA: Um, sure we do.

MOWGLI: We are going to drive these buffalo and trample Shere Khan to death!

AKELA: Sounds good. Very realistic.

MOWGLI: Watch, I will get them to practice stampeding *(demonstrates to audience to practice "stampeding" by stomping their feet down)*

MOWGLI: *(calls offstage)* Hey!! Shere Khan! Come out, come out wherever you are!

(enter SHERE KHAN)

SHERE KHAN: Who calls? *(gasps)* It's you. Finally, the time has come! Muahahahahaha! ROAR!

MOWGLI: *(to AKELA and BAGHERRA)* Go! *(MOWGLI, BAGHEERA and AKELA get the audience to start stampeding with their hands and feet in big motions.)*

SHERE KHAN: NOOOOO! Trampled to death by buffalo! *(to audience)* Very realistic! AGHHHHHHH!!! *(Shere Khan now falls to the ground and rolls around melodramatically, finally dying)*

MOWGLI: Ha ha! It is all over.

(enter MESSUA)

MESSUA: What is this folly! You didn't kill this tiger all by yourself, did you?

MOWGLI: No, they helped. *(he casually throws his arms around AKELA and BAGHEERA).* Nice work, friends! *(MOWGLI, AKELA and BAGHEERA high five each other and laugh together)*

MESSUA: Wait, you can talk to animals?! This is a problem, the villiagers will call you: "Sorcerer! Wolf's brat! Jungle demon!"

MOWGLI: Whoa! Why, what is this? Did I do something wrong?

MESSUA: Oh, my son, go away or they will kill thee. Villagers are really scared of little boys who talk to animals. It was nice knowing you Nathoo...Mowgli... whatever your name is. Bye! *(MESSUA exits)*

MOWGLI: Fare you well, children of men! I'm outta here. *(to AKELA and BAGHEERA)* Come on guys, let's go back to the jungle.

(ALL exit)

ACT 2 SCENE 4

(enter MOWGLI, AKELA, PARENT WOLF, BAGHEERA, BALOO, and WOLVES)

MOWGLI: *(to PARENT WOLF)* They have cast me out from the Man-Pack, but it's okay because we killed Shere Khan!

(SHERE KHAN enters and dies again; all the WOLVES give a big "hooray!")

PARENT WOLF: Nice work, Little Frog. I'm proud of you.

BAGHEERA: We were lonely in the jungle without thee.

MOWGLI: Aw, shucks. I missed you guys too.

BALOO: Gross, this is getting way too sappy.

AKELA: Lead us again, O Man-cub!

BAGHEERA: No way. Ye fought for freedom, and it is yours. Eat it, O Wolves.

MOWGLI: I think I like being free. I don't want to belong to any pack! Now I will hunt alone in the jungle.

AKELA: And we will hunt with thee.

MOWGLI: I said 'alone' didn't I? Oh well, it's good to have friends. I'm hungry...let's hunt!

ALL: HOWL!!!!!

(ALL exit running)

THE END

The 20-Minute or so The Jungle Book for Kids

By Rudyard Kipling

Creatively modified by

Khara C. Barnhart and Brendan P. Kelso

9-12+ Actors

CAST OF CHARACTERS:

MOWGLI: random human boy living in the jungle

PARENT WOLF: Mowgli's wolf parent

GRAY BROTHER: Mowgli's wolf brother

SHERE KHAN: tiger who wants to eat Mowgli for lunch!

[1]**BALOO:** a bear who teaches Mowgli the Laws of the Jungle

BAGHEERA: a panther who looks out for Mowgli

[3]**KAA:** a hungry, old and powerful python

[3]**AKELA:** leader of the wolf pack

RIKKI-TIKKI TAVI: a mongoose, master snake killer

[2]**NAGAINA:** a cobra who enjoys eating humans

[2]**MESSUA:** Mowgli's adopted human mom

[1]**BULDEO:** village hunter and a coward

Any extras can be:

MONKEY-PEOPLE: vain, silly animals (all actors not onstage in a different role play MONKEY-PEOPLE)

WOLVES: More than one wolf (all actors not onstage in a different role play WOLVES)

BUFFALO: the audience!

The same actors can play the following parts:

[1]BALOO and BULDEO

[2]NAGAINA and MESSUA

[3]KAA and AKELA

(enter BAGHEERA, PARENT WOLF, and GRAY BROTHER)

PARENT WOLF: Augrh! It is time to hunt again!

GRAY BROTHER: Hurry up, I'm hungry! We wolves have to eat! *(howls)*

(enter BAGHEERA)

BAGHEERA: Good luck go with you, O Chief of the Wolves!

PARENT WOLF: Oh hi, Bagheera. What's happening in the life of a panther?

BAGHEERA: I wanted to warn you. Shere Khan's in town again.

PARENT WOLF: The tiger? What's he doing in this part of the jungle?

BAGHEERA: What tigers do. You know, hunt, eat, hunt again, eat... hunt....eat... *(trailing off)*

PARENT WOLF: *(play-acting like a tiger)* Oh look at me, I'm a mean ol' tiger, roar!!!

GRAY BROTHER: WOW! You're good! *(there is a LOUD ROAR from offstage, PARENT WOLF is a bit shocked)*

BAGHEERA: Listen! That's him now! *(enter MOWGLI, running off-balance, and falling down)*

PARENT WOLF: Whoa! A man's cub! Look! *(ALL turn to look at MOWGLI)* How little and so... smelly, but cute! *(starts petting his hair)*

(BAGHEERA sneaks over to MOWGLI and whispers something in his ear. MOWGLI sighs and gets down on his knees to appear smaller; he remains on his knees throughout the rest of the scene and ACT1 SCENE 2)

MOWGLI: *(very sarcastically)* Gaa gaa. Goo goo.

(SHERE KHAN enters. PARENT WOLF hides MOWGLI behind back)

SHERE KHAN: A man's cub went this way. Its parents have run off. Give it to me. I'll uh...take care of him... *(as he rubs his belly)* you can TOTALLY trust me! *(gives the audience a big evil smile)*

PARENT WOLF: You are NOT the boss of us.

SHERE KHAN: Excuse me?! Do you know who I am? It is I, Shere Khan, who speaks! I'm kind of a big deal. And scary! GRRRRR.

PARENT WOLF: The man's cub is mine; he shall not be killed! So beat it; you don't scare us.

SHERE KHAN: Fine. But I'll get him some day, make no mistake! Muahahahahaha! ROAR! *(SHERE KHAN exits)*

PARENT WOLF: *(to MOWGLI)* Mowgli the Frog I will call thee. Lie still, little frog.

GRAY BROTHER: *(to PARENT WOLF)* I thought he was a man-cub?

MOWGLI: *(to GRAY BROTHER)* Frog?

GRAY BROTHER: *(to MOWGLI and audience)* Don't ask me, I'm just a kid! What can I say, parents are strange. Right?

(MOWGLI nods; ALL stay on stage)

ACT 1 SCENE 2

(enter AKELA, BALOO, BAGHEERA, and WOLVES)

AKELA: Okay, wolves, let's get this meeting started! Howl!

WOLVES: Howl!!! *(All WOLVES howl, but one WOLF crows like a Rooster, coughs, then howls. All look at him strangely)*

PARENT WOLF: Akela, our great leader, I'd like to present the newest member of our pack, Mowgli the Frog!

AKELA: Hmmm, Frog, huh? If you say so. *(to WOLVES)* Is everyone good with this? *(WOLVES begin howling)*

(enter SHERE KHAN)

SHERE KHAN: ROAR! The cub is mine! Give him to me!

AKELA: Who speaks for this cub?

BALOO: *(speaking in a big, deep bear voice!)* I, Baloo the Bear, I speak for the man's cub. I myself will teach him the ways of the jungle.

BAGHEERA: I know I'm a panther, not a wolf, but if the pack takes him in, I'll provide you with a fat bull for your party. You guys like bull, right?

WOLVES: Yeah! Yum! We love bull! *(same WOLF as earlier yells "Chicken!" All look at him strangely again)*

AKELA: Yeah! Cool, then it's settled. The panther, the bear, and us wolves will look out for the man-cub. *(high fives MOWGLI)* Guess that makes us man-cub's best friend!

MOWGLI: *(sarcastically)* Gaa gaa. Goo goo.

SHERE KHAN: Fine! *(begins to exit and mumbles to audience while shaking fist)* I would have gotten him too, if it weren't for those meddling jungle creatures! But I'll get him someday. Muahahahahaha! ROAR!

(enter RIKKI-TIKKI, chasing NAGAINA)

RIKKI-TIKKI: *(to NAGAINA)* Halt there, cobra! Stay and fight with honor! *(RIKKI-TIKKI does a bunch of exaggerated karate moves)* Rikk-tikk-tikki-tikki-tchk!

BAGHEERA: Rikki, What are you doing here? This is NOT your play!

NAGAINA: *(notices audience)* Ooooo! Sssssssssweet, sssssssweet humans! I'm going to eat them! *(She begins wiggling towards audience, hissing)*

RIKKI-TIKKI: *(to BAGHEERA)* Yeah, I know, but it looked like fun being on stage. *(sees cobra approaching audience)* Nooooo! *(starts chasing NAGAINA)* We need the audience...for now...

AKELA: Hey guys? GUYS!? Mongoose, Cobra!!! *(RIKKI-TIKKI and NAGAINA stop and look at AKELA)* Um, wrong story. Do you mind?

RIKKI-TIKKI: Okay, okay, we'll leave. *(attacking NAGAINA)* HI-YA! *(loudly)* Rikk-tikk-tikki-tikki-tchk! *(chases NAGAINA offstage)*

BAGHEERA: Silly little mongoose.

PARENT WOLF: Now, where were we?

AKELA: Oh, the man cub. He can join the pack. Take him away and train him as befits one of the Free People. Come on wolves; there's a fat bull calling our names!

(ALL exit howling)

(enter BALOO and BAGHEERA)

BALOO: *(noticing BAGHEERA)* Checking up on me, eh?

BAGHEERA: Just want to make sure Mowgli's lessons are you know, actually happening. It has been some years since he came and joined the pack.

BALOO: I've been his teacher for all these years, and you still don't trust me? Fine. I've taught him how to tell a rotten branch from a sound one, how to speak politely to the wild bees, and the Stranger's Hunting Call. You know, the bare necessities!

BAGHEERA: Well, don't overdo it.

BALOO: Look, the jungle is a SUPER dangerous place. He needs to know all this stuff.

BAGHEERA: And remember, you're a bear, so be gentle with him!

BALOO: That's right, I AM a bear who TALKS. This story takes place in the JUNGLE. I am standing here talking to a PANTHER, and I spend my days teaching a HUMAN. If you hadn't noticed, none of this makes sense.

BAGHEERA: Huh...very true. Carry on.

(enter MOWGLI)

BALOO: Mowgli, show Bagheera what I've taught you. What do you say to the animal hunters in the jungle?

MOWGLI: *(loudly, with a low booming voice)* We be of one blood, ye and I.

BALOO: And to the birds?

MOWGLI: *(flaps arms like a bird)* Kaaaaaa! Kaaaaaaaaaaa!

BALOO: And the Snake-People?

MOWGLI: *(wiggles on his belly)* Hissssssssssss Hissssssssssss *(darts tongue in and out of mouth)*

BAGHEERA: Amazing.

BALOO: Right? *(nodding head)*

MOWGLI: Yeah, and someday I shall have a tribe of my own, and lead them through the branches all day long!

BALOO: Wait, what? Tribe?

BAGHEERA: Branches?

BALOO and BAGHEERA: The Monkey-People!

MOWGLI: They're super cool! They said I was their blood brother, except that I had no tail, and should be their leader some day!

BAGHEERA: They have no leader. They lie. They have always lied. They will throw... stuff at you!

BALOO: Listen, man-cub. Those monkeys...they are outcasts. We do not drink where the monkeys drink; we do not go where the monkeys go; we do not hunt where they hunt...

MOWGLI: Come on, Baloo. *(mimics BALOO's voice and actions melodramatically)* We do not HUNT where they HUNT...

BAGHEERA: Dude, this is serious jungle stuff.

MOWGLI: Fine. No monkey business. *(chuckles to audience)*

BALOO: I think it's naptime.

BAGHEERA: Good idea.

(all three lie down onstage and fall asleep. Enter MONKEYS. They grab MOWGLI and run in a large circle and take him offstage while making lots of monkey noises. BALOO and BAGHEERA wake up to see the MONKEYS taking MOWGLI away)

MOWGLI: They've kidnapped me! Mark my trail! Help!

BALOO: Noooooooooooo! I can't believe I let them take him! Roll me into the hives of the wild bees that I may be stung to death, for I am the most miserable of bears! *(BALOO lies down on the floor and starts moaning and crying)*

BAGHEERA: Oh, get over yourself. This is NOT helping.

BALOO: *(stops crying)* I know, let's get Kaa!

BAGHEERA: The python?

BALOO: He is very old and very cunning. Above all, he is very hungry. Promise him many goats. No one can resist goats.

BAGHEERA: Goats? It's worth a shot, I guess. Let's go. *(BALOO and BAGHEERA begin walking around the stage; enter KAA)*

BALOO: There he is. *(to KAA)* Good hunting!

BAGHEERA: He's super old and can't hear well, remember?

BALOO: Oh right. Ahem. *(yells)* GOOOOOD HUUUUNTING, Kaa!! *(waves arms)*

KAA: I'm ssssssuper hungry.

BAGHEERA: Of course you are, you old snake. *(KAA doesn't hear)*

BALOO: *(loudly and slow)* We are hunting...the MONKEY-PEOPLE.

KAA: What? Those chattering, foolish, vain, Monkey-People. I can't sssssssstand them.

BAGHEERA: *(loudly)* They have stolen away our man-cub.

KAA: Monkeyssss are thievessssss! Let'ssss get them! Where'd they go?

BALOO and BAGHEERA: That way. *(they point in different directions)*

KAA: Brilliant. Well, let'sssssss try the monkey city.

BALOO: Ssssounds good.

BAGHEERA: We need to hurry...let's run! *(looks at KAA and yells)* Er, sssslither!

(ALL exit)

(enter MOWGLI and MONKEYS. MONKEYS are having a party and making a mess; throwing bananas around, dancing and making lots of monkey noises. Every time MOWGLI tries to leave, a MONKEY pulls him back to center stage)

MONKEYS: *(chanting)* We are great! We are free! We are wonderful! We are the most wonderful people in all the jungle!

MOWGLI: You are full of yourselves.

MONKEYS: We all say so, so it must be true! Teach us how to make shelters from sticks and canes like men do!

MOWGLI: Um, I live with wolves, remember? In a cave! *(to audience)* These monkeys are crazy. *(MOWGLI sits center stage with the MONKEYS forming a circle around him. They tickle him, push him, and laugh at each other)*

(enter BAGHEERA, BALOO and KAA, tiptoeing up to the MONKEYS. They attack MONKEYS from all sides. MOWGLI is tugged between MONKEYS and BALOO. Finally KAA gives a very loud and fierce HISSSSSSSS, and the MONKEYS run offstage, scared)

BAGHEERA: Let us take the man-cub and go before they come back!

KAA: They won't come back. I'm pretty sssscary. Hissssssssssss......

BALOO: Wow, I am sore. *(to MOWGLI)* Art thou hurt?

MOWGLI: No. *(pause; makes fun of BALOO)* I art hungry!

KAA: A boy after my own heart!

MOWGLI: *(to KAA)* We be one blood, thou and I. Let'ssss go get some goatssss!

KAA: Now you're talking! I love goatssssssss!

BALOO: *(to BAGHEERA)* Ssssee, I told you goatsssss would work.

(ALL exit)

ACT 2 SCENE 1

(enter BAGHEERA and MOWGLI)

BAGHEERA: Little Brother, how often have I told thee that Shere Khan is thy enemy?

MOWGLI: Not this again! I know, I know, he wants to kill me and eat me for lunch! But why? Why should any wish to kill me?

BAGHEERA: Because, Shere Khan is a hungry tiger! And 'cause you're a human. In case you forgot. Sort of a delicacy.

MOWGLI: Well, that's just not cool. **BAGHEERA:** You know what you need for protection? The Red Flower! You should go and get some from the man village.

MOWGLI: How is a flower supposed to protect me?

BAGHEERA: It's not really a flower. That's just what we call it. It's FIRE!

MOWGLI: Well that makes more sense. I'll go get some. *(MOWGLI exits; RIKKI-TIKKI and NAGAINA pass him as they enter, running)*

RIKKI-TIKKI: Turn round, Nagaina. Turn and fight! *(RIKKI-TIKKI once again poses in a karate stance)*

NAGAINA: *(noticing audience)* Look at your friendssss, Rikki-tikki! They are funny looking and sssssmell delicioussssss! They are afraid. Better for me to eat them. *(she hisses and starts moving towards the audience)*

RIKKI-TIKKI: I'll destroy you just like I destroyed your husband! Oh, and did I forget to tell you that I smashed all your eggs? 'Cause I totally did. Come fight me. You shall not be a widow long! *(NAGAINA stops and turns towards RIKKI-TIKKI)*

NAGAINA: You're dead, mongoossssse! *(she mimics RIKKI-TIKKI's karate pose; they fight but do not actually touch each other)*

RIKKI-TIKKI: Rikki-tikki-tch-tch! HI-YA! *(RIKKI-TIKKI karate chops NAGAINA and she dies melodramatically)*

BAGHEERA: *(doing a slow clap)* Bravo, Rikki-Tikki, bravo. But could you move along? What did I say earlier?

RIKKI-TIKKI: I know, I know, "It's not my play." Way to ruin the moment. *(to audience, sarcastically)* You're welcome! *(RIKKI-TIKKI drags NAGAINA offstage)*

(enter MOWGLI holding a pot)

MOWGLI: Got the fire...er, I mean, flower! *(winks to audience)*

BAGHEERA: Just in time...

(MOWGLI and BAGHEERA stay on stage)

ACT 2 SCENE 2

(enter AKELA, SHERE KHAN, PARENT WOLF, GRAY BROTHER, and WOLVES)

SHERE KHAN: Akela, your time as leader of the wolves is over.

PARENT WOLF: Akela has been an awesome leader, Shere Khan.

SHERE KHAN: Bah! What do we have to do with this toothless fool! He is doomed to die!

AKELA: Hey man, not cool! I'm not toothless.

SHERE KHAN: It is the man-cub who has lived too long. Free People, he was my meat from the first. Give him to me!

WOLVES: Yeah! He stinks too! Give him to the tiger!

AKELA: Chill out, guys. He is our brother in all but blood, and ye would kill him here! You're all cowards!

WOLVES: Boo! He is a man! *(pointing at MOWGLI)* Get lost, man-cub!

BAGHEERA: *(to MOWGLI)* I think now's the time...

MOWGLI: You keep saying that "I am a man", so I guess instead of brothers, I need to call you dogs. And guess what? Dogs are scared of fire, aren't they? *(MOWGLI runs around to the WOLVES and SHERE KHAN and shakes the pot of fire in their faces. They all fling themselves to the ground in terror)*

SHERE KHAN: It burns! Oh how it burns!!

MOWGLI: Serves you right! Now I will go to men. I'm done with the jungle. *(walks over to PARENT WOLF and GRAY BROTHER)* Ye will not forget me?

GRAY BROTHER: Never!

PARENT WOLF: Come soon! We be old, thy mother and I. I loved thee more than ever I loved my cubs.

GRAY BROTHER: *(sarcastically to PARENT WOLF)* Hey, I'm standing right here!

MOWGLI: I'll come back once I've killed Shere Khan. Do not forget me! Tell them in the jungle never to forget me!

SHERE KHAN: *(to self)* I won't forget you Mowgli! *(does an evil, evil laugh!)* Muahahahahaha! ROAR!

(ALL exit)

(enter MOWGLI and MESSUA with BULDEO from opposite side of the stage)

MOWGLI: *(pointing at audience)* Look, humans! *(calls out)* We be of one blood, ye and I! *(to audience)* Oh wait, you probably don't speak jungle, do you?

MESSUA: Look, Buldeo, a random wild boy!

BULDEO: Hmmm. Perhaps a wolf-child run away from the jungle? Hey, Messua, he looks like your son that was taken by the tiger a long time ago. The one with the weird name.

MESSUA: Holy cow! He does! *(to MOWGLI)* Nathoo! Nathoo!

MOWGLI: Bless you. By the way. I'm Mowgli.

MESSUA: Great! How did you learn how to speak?

MOWGLI: From a bear and a panther.

MESSUA: Oh...that's strange. Anyway, you're going to be my replacement son! *(she hugs him)*

MOWGLI: Hmmm, a bit weird, but, okay!

BULDEO: Welcome to our village, little wolf-dude.

(enter GRAY BROTHER)

GRAY BROTHER: Psssssst! Hey, Mowgli!

MOWGLI: *(to MESSUA and BULDEO)* I'll be right back. *(runs to GRAY BROTHER)* Hey brother, what's up?

GRAY BROTHER: Just wanted to let you know that, *(sniffs and plugs nose)* phew, you smell gross! Where was I... oh yeah, Shere Khan still wants to kill you.

MOWGLI: Thanks for the warning. Let me know when he gets close. *(runs back to MESSUA and BULDEO; GRAY BROTHER exits)*

BULDEO: Okay, look. Everyone has a job here, even the kids. You can go watch the buffalo graze in the field. *(points at the audience implying they are the buffalo)* Cool?

MOWGLI: Cool.

MESSUA: Be safe, Nathoo...Mowgli...whatever your name is. Bye! *(MESSUA and BULDEO exit; MOWGLI sits down)*

MOWGLI: Watching buffalo is booooring.

(enter GRAY BROTHER AND AKELA)

GRAY BROTHER: Shere Khan is back, Mowgli! He's waiting for you in the ravine!

MOWGLI: *(jumps up)* Awesome. I am not afraid of Shere Khan. We have big work in hand. I have an idea, see all these buffalo? *(he gestures to the audience)*

AKELA: *(sarcastically)* Um, sure we do.

MOWGLI: We are going to drive these buffalo and trample Shere Khan to death!

AKELA: Sounds good. Very realistic.

MOWGLI: Watch, I will get them to practice stampeding *(demonstrates to audience to practice "stampeding" by stomping their feet down)*

MOWGLI: *(calls offstage)* Hey!! Shere Khan! Come out, come out wherever you are!

(enter SHERE KHAN)

SHERE KHAN: Who calls? *(gasps)* It's you. Finally, the time has come! Muahahahahaha! ROAR!

MOWGLI: *(to AKELA and GRAY BROTHER)* Go! *(MOWGLI, GRAY BROTHER and AKELA get the audience to start stampeding with their hands and feet in big motions.)*

SHERE KHAN: NOOOOO! Trampled to death by buffalo! *(to audience)* Very realistic! AGHHHHHHH!!! *(Shere Khan now falls to the ground and rolls around melodramatically, finally dying)*

MOWGLI: Ha ha! It is all over.

(enter BULDEO and MESSUA)

BULDEO: What is this folly! You didn't kill this tiger all by yourself, did you?

MOWGLI: No, they helped. *(he casually throws his arms around AKELA and GRAY BROTHER).* Nice work, friends! *(MOWGLI, AKELA and GRAY BROTHER high five each other and laugh together)*

BULDEO: Wait, you can talk to animals?! *(suddenly VERY scared)* Sorcerer! Wolf's brat! Jungle demon! Go away!

MOWGLI: Whoa! Now what is this? Did I do something wrong?

MESSUA: Oh, my son, go away or Buldeo will kill thee. Villagers are really scared of little boys who talk to animals. It was nice knowing you Nathoo...Mowgli... whatever your name is. Bye! *(MESSUA exits)*

MOWGLI: Fare you well, children of men! I'm outta here. *(to AKELA and GRAY BROTHER)* Come on guys, let's go back to the jungle.

(ALL exit)

ACT 2 SCENE 4

(enter MOWGLI, AKELA, GRAY BROTHER, PARENT WOLF, BAGHEERA, BALOO, and WOLVES)

MOWGLI: *(to PARENT WOLF)* They have cast me out from the Man-Pack, but it's okay because we killed Shere Khan!

(SHERE KHAN enters and dies again; all the WOLVES give a big "hooray!")

PARENT WOLF: Nice work, Little Frog. I'm proud of you.

BAGHEERA: We were lonely in the jungle without thee.

MOWGLI: Aw, shucks. I missed you guys too.

BALOO: Gross, this is getting way too sappy.

WOLVES: Lead us again, O Akela. Lead us again, O Man-cub!

BAGHEERA: No way. Ye fought for freedom, and it is yours. Eat it, O Wolves.

MOWGLI: I think I like being free. I don't want to belong to any pack! Now I will hunt alone in the jungle.

ALL WOLVES: And we will hunt with thee.

MOWGLI: I said 'alone' didn't I? Oh well, it's good to have friends. I'm hungry...let's hunt!

ALL: HOWL!!!!!

(ALL exit running)

THE END

NOTES

The 25-Minute or so
The Jungle Book for Kids
By Rudyard Kipling
Creatively modified by
Khara C. Barnhart and Brendan P. Kelso
13-16+ Actors

CAST OF CHARACTERS:

MOWGLI: random human boy living in the jungle

[1]**FATHER WOLF:** Mowgli's wolf dad

[2]**MOTHER WOLF:** Mowgli's wolf mom

GRAY BROTHER: Mowgli's wolf brother

TABAQUI: sneaky, gossipy jackal

SHERE KHAN: tiger who wants to eat Mowgli for lunch!

BALOO: a bear who teaches Mowgli the Laws of the Jungle

BAGHEERA: a panther who looks out for Mowgli

[3]**KAA:** a hungry, old and powerful python

[3]**AKELA:** leader of the wolf pack

RANN THE KITE: bird who helps Mowgli

RIKKI-TIKKI TAVI: a mongoose, master snake killer

NAG: a human eating cobra

NAGAINA: Nag's wife, also enjoys eating humans

[2]**MESSUA:** Mowgli's adopted human mom

[1]**BULDEO:** village hunter and a coward

Any extras can be:

MONKEY-PEOPLE: vain, silly animals (all actors not onstage in a different role play MONKEY-PEOPLE)

WOLVES: More than one wolf (all actors not onstage in a different role play WOLVES)

BUFFALO: the audience!

The same actors can play the following parts:

[1]FATHER WOLF and BULDEO

[2]MOTHER WOLF and MESSUA

[3]KAA and AKELA

ACT 1 SCENE 1

(enter FATHER WOLF, MOTHER WOLF, and GRAY BROTHER)

FATHER WOLF: Augrh! It is time to hunt again!

GRAY BROTHER: Hurry up, Dad. I'm hungry! We wolves have to eat! *(howls)*

(enter TABAQUI)

TABAQUI: Good luck go with you, O Chief of the Wolves!

MOTHER WOLF: Ugh, Tabaqui, you jackal, what do you want? There is no food here.

TABAQUI: Hey, can't a jackal just make a friendly visit to the wolves? So, have you heard the big news? Shere Khan's in town again.

MOTHER WOLF: The tiger? What's he doing in this part of the jungle?

TABAQUI: What tigers do. You know, hunt, eat, hunt again, eat... hunt....eat... *(trailing off)*

MOTHER WOLF: *(play-acting like a tiger)* Oh look at me, I'm a mean ol' tiger, roar!!!

GRAY BROTHER: WOW Mom! You're good! *(there is a LOUD ROAR from offstage, MOTHER WOLF is a bit shocked)*

TABAQUI: Listen! That's him now!

(enter MOWGLI, running off-balance, and falling down)

FATHER WOLF: Whoa! A man's cub! Look! *(ALL turn to look at MOWGLI)*

MOTHER WOLF: How little and so... smelly, but cute! *(starts petting his hair)*

(TABAQUI sneaks over to MOWGLI and whispers something in his ear. MOWGLI sighs and gets down on his knees to appear smaller; he remains on his knees throughout the rest of the scene and ACT1 SCENE 2)

MOWGLI: *(very sarcastically)* Gaa gaa. Goo goo.

(SHERE KHAN enters. MOTHER WOLF hides MOWGLI behind her back)

SHERE KHAN: A man's cub went this way. Its parents have run off. Give it to me. I'll uh...take care of him... *(as he rubs his belly)* you can TOTALLY trust me! *(gives the audience a big evil smile)*

FATHER WOLF: You are NOT the boss of us.

SHERE KHAN: Excuse me?! Do you know who I am? It is I, Shere Khan, who speaks! I'm kind of a big deal. And scary! GRRRRR.

MOTHER WOLF: The man's cub is mine; he shall not be killed! So beat it; you don't scare us.

SHERE KHAN: Fine. But I'll get him some day, make no mistake! Muahahahahaha! ROAR! *(SHERE KHAN exits with TABAQUI following)*

MOTHER WOLF: *(to MOWGLI)* Mowgli the Frog I will call thee. Lie still, little frog.

GRAY BROTHER: *(to FATHER WOLF)* I thought he was a man-cub?

MOWGLI: *(to FATHER WOLF)* Frog?

FATHER WOLF: *(to MOWGLI and audience)* She's the mom. Happy wife, happy life, right? If she wants to name you frog, so be it! But now we have to see what the pack says.

(ALL stay on stage)

ACT 1 SCENE 2

(enter AKELA, BALOO, BAGHEERA, and WOLVES)

AKELA: Okay, wolves, let's get this meeting started! Howl!

WOLVES: Howl!! *(All WOLVES howl, but one WOLF crows like a Rooster, coughs, then howls. All look at him weird)*

MOTHER WOLF: Akela, our great leader, I'd like to present the newest member of our pack, Mowgli the Frog!

AKELA: Hmmm, Frog, huh? If you say so. *(to WOLVES)* Is everyone good with this? *(WOLVES begin howling)*

(enter SHERE KHAN)

SHERE KHAN: ROAR! The cub is mine! Give him to me!

AKELA: Who speaks for this cub?

BALOO: *(speaking in a big, deep bear voice!)* I, Baloo the Bear, I speak for the man's cub. I myself will teach him the ways of the jungle.

BAGHEERA: I know I'm a panther, not a wolf, but if the pack takes him in, I'll provide you with a fat bull for your party. You guys like bull, right?

WOLVES: Yeah! Yum! We love bull! *(same WOLF as earlier yells "Chicken!" All look at him weird again)*

AKELA: Yeah! Cool, then it's settled. The panther, the bear, and us wolves will look out for the man-cub. *(high fives MOWGLI)* Guess that makes us man-cub's best friend!

MOWGLI: *(sarcastically)* Gaa gaa. Goo goo.

SHERE KHAN: Fine! *(begins to exit and mumbles to audience while shaking fist)* I would have gotten him too, if it weren't for those meddling jungle creatures! But I'll get him someday. Muahahahahaha! ROAR!

(enter RIKKI-TIKKI, chasing NAG and NAGAINA)

RIKKI-TIKKI: *(to NAG and NAGAINA)* Halt there, cobras! Stay and fight with honor! *(RIKKI-TIKKI does a bunch of exaggerated karate moves)* Rikk-tikk-tikki-tikki-tchk!

BAGHEERA: Rikki, What are you doing here? This is NOT your play!

NAG: *(notices audience. To NAGAINA)* Look, Nagaina! Humansssssss!

NAGAINA: Ooooo! Sssssssssweet, ssssssssweet humans! Let'ssssss eat them!

NAG: Good idea! Hssssssss. *(they begin wiggling towards audience, hissing)*

RIKKI-TIKKI: *(to BAGHEERA)* Yeah, I know, but it looked like fun being on stage. *(sees cobras approaching audience)* Nooooo! *(starts chasing NAG and NAGAINA)* We need the audience...for now...

AKELA: Hey guys? GUYS!? Mongoose, Cobras!!! *(RIKKI-TIKKI, NAG and NAGAINA stop and look at AKELA)* Um, wrong story. Do you mind?

RIKKI-TIKKI: Okay, okay, we'll leave. *(attacking cobras)* HI-YA! *(loudly)* Rikk-tikk-tikki-tikki-tchk! *(chases NAG and NAGAINA offstage)*

BAGHEERA: Silly little mongoose.

FATHER WOLF: Now, where were we?

AKELA: Oh, the man cub. He can join the pack. Take him away and train him as befits one of the Free People. Come on wolves; there's a fat bull calling our names!

(ALL exit howling)

(enter BALOO and BAGHEERA)

BALOO: *(noticing BAGHEERA)* Checking up on me, eh?

BAGHEERA: Just want to make sure Mowgli's lessons are you know, actually happening. It has been some years since he came and joined the pack.

BALOO: I've been his teacher for all these years, and you still don't trust me? Fine. I've taught him how to tell a rotten branch from a sound one, how to speak politely to the wild bees, and the Stranger's Hunting Call. You know, the bare necessities!

BAGHEERA: Well, don't overdo it.

BALOO: Look, the jungle is a SUPER dangerous place. He needs to know all this stuff.

BAGHEERA: And remember, you're a bear, so be gentle with him!

BALOO: That's right, I AM a bear who TALKS. This story takes place in the JUNGLE. I am standing here talking to a PANTHER, and I spend my days teaching a HUMAN. If you hadn't noticed, none of this makes sense.

BAGHEERA: Huh...very true. Carry on.

(enter MOWGLI)

BALOO: Mowgli, show Bagheera what I've taught you. What do you say to the animal hunters in the jungle?

MOWGLI: *(loudly, with a low booming voice)* We be of one blood, ye and I.

BALOO: And to the birds?

MOWGLI: *(flaps arms like a bird)* Kaaaaaa! Kaaaaaaaaaaa!

BALOO: And the Snake-People?

MOWGLI: *(wiggles on his belly)* Hissssssssssss Hisssssssssss *(darts tongue in and out of mouth)*

BAGHEERA: Amazing.

BALOO: Right? *(nodding head)*

MOWGLI: Yeah, and someday I shall have a tribe of my own, and lead them through the branches all day long!

BALOO: Wait, what? Tribe?

BAGHEERA: Branches?

BALOO and BAGHEERA: The Monkey-People!

MOWGLI: They're super cool! They said I was their blood brother, except that I had no tail, and should be their leader some day!

BAGHEERA: They have no leader. They lie. They have always lied. They will throw... stuff at you!

BALOO: Listen, man-cub. Those monkeys...they are outcasts. We do not drink where the monkeys drink; we do not go where the monkeys go; we do not hunt where they hunt...

MOWGLI: Come on, Baloo. *(mimics BALOO's voice and actions melodramatically)* We do not HUNT where they HUNT...

BAGHEERA: Dude, this is serious jungle stuff.

MOWGLI: Fine. No monkey business. *(chuckles to audience)*

BALOO: I think it's naptime.

BAGHEERA: Good idea.

(all three lie down onstage and fall asleep. Enter MONKEYS. They grab MOWGLI and run in a large circle and take him offstage while making lots of monkey noises. BALOO and BAGHEERA wake up to see the MONKEYS taking MOWGLI away)

BALOO: Noooooooooooo! *(BALOO and BAGHEERA run offstage just as MOWGLI and the MONKEYS run onstage on the opposite side of the stage; enter RANN, flapping wings)*

MOWGLI: Rann!! Hey Rann!

RANN: Do I know you, little man? You don't look like you belong with the monkeys.

MOWGLI: They've kidnapped me! Mark my trail! Tell Baloo and Bagheera.

RANN: In whose name, brother?

MOWGLI: Mowgli, the Frog! Man-cub they call me!

RANN: Groovy! You can count on me! *(exit MOWGLI, MONKEYS and RANN; enter BALOO and BAGHEERA)*

BALOO: I can't believe I let them take him! Roll me into the hives of the wild bees that I may be stung to death, for I am the most miserable of bears! *(BALOO lies down on the floor and starts moaning and crying)*

BAGHEERA: Oh, get over yourself. This is NOT helping.

BALOO: *(stops crying)* I know, let's get Kaa!

BAGHEERA: The python?

BALOO: He is very old and very cunning. Above all, he is very hungry. Promise him many goats. No one can resist goats.

BAGHEERA: Goats? It's worth a shot, I guess. Let's go. *(BALOO and BAGHEERA begin walking around the stage; enter KAA)*

BALOO: There he is. *(to KAA)* Good hunting!

BAGHEERA: He's super old and can't hear well, remember?

BALOO: Oh right. Ahem. *(yells)* GOOOOOD HUUUUNTING, Kaa!! *(waves arms)*

KAA: I'm sssssssuper hungry.

BAGHEERA: Of course you are, you old snake. *(KAA doesn't hear)*

BALOO: *(loudly and slow)* We are hunting...the MONKEY-PEOPLE.

KAA: What? Those chattering, foolish, vain, Monkey-People. I can't ssssssssstand them.

BAGHEERA: *(loudly)* They have stolen away our man-cub.

KAA: Monkeys are thievessssss! Let'ssss get them! Where'd they go?

BALOO and BAGHEERA: That way. *(they point in different directions)*

KAA: Brilliant.

(enter RANN, flying around stage)

RANN: Baloooooooo! Bagheeeeeeeeeraaaaaaaaaaa!

BALOO: *(to RANN)* What is it, Rann the Kite?

RANN: I have seen Mowgli among the Monkey-People. They have taken him beyond the river to the monkey city! That is my message. See ya! *(RANN exits)*

BAGHEERA: You heard the bird. Let's fly...I mean run! *(looks at KAA and yells)* Er, sssslither! Whatever!

(ALL exit)

(enter MOWGLI and MONKEYS. MONKEYS are having a party and making a mess; throwing bananas around, dancing and making lots of monkey noises. Every time MOWGLI tries to leave, a MONKEY pulls him back to center stage)

MONKEYS: *(chanting)* We are great! We are free! We are wonderful! We are the most wonderful people in all the jungle!

MOWGLI: You are full of yourselves.

MONKEYS: We all say so, so it must be true! Teach us how to make shelters from sticks and canes like men do!

MOWGLI: Um, I live with wolves, remember? In a cave! *(to audience)* These monkeys are crazy. *(MOWGLI sits center stage with the MONKEYS forming a circle around him. They tickle him, push him, and laugh at each other)*

(enter BAGHEERA, BALOO and KAA, tiptoeing up to the MONKEYS. They attack MONKEYS from all sides. MOWGLI is tugged between MONKEYS and BALOO. Finally KAA gives a very loud and fierce HISSSSSSSS, and the MONKEYS run offstage, scared)

BAGHEERA: Let us take the man-cub and go before they come back!

KAA: They won't come back. I'm pretty sssscary. Hissssssssssss......

BALOO: Wow, I am sore. *(to MOWGLI)* Art thou hurt?

MOWGLI: No. *(pause; makes fun of BALOO)* I art hungry!

KAA: A boy after my own heart!

MOWGLI: *(to KAA)* We be one blood, thou and I. Let'ssss go get some goatsssss!

KAA: Now you're talking! I love goatsssssss!

BALOO: *(to BAGHEERA)* Ssssee, I told you goatssss would work.

(ALL exit)

(enter BAGHEERA and MOWGLI)

BAGHEERA: Little Brother, how often have I told thee that Shere Khan is thy enemy?

MOWGLI: Not this again! I know, I know, he wants to kill me and eat me for lunch! But why? Why should any wish to kill me?

BAGHEERA: Because, Shere Khan is a hungry tiger! And 'cause you're a human. In case you forgot. Sort of a delicacy.

MOWGLI: Well, that's just not cool.

BAGHEERA: You know what you need for protection? The Red Flower! You should go and get some from the man village.

MOWGLI: How is a flower supposed to protect me?

BAGHEERA: It's not really a flower. That's just what we call it. It's FIRE!

MOWGLI: Well that makes more sense. I'll go get some.

(MOWGLI exits)

(RIKKI-TIKKI and NAGAINA enter, running)

RIKKI-TIKKI: Turn round, Nagaina. Turn and fight!
(RIKKI-TIKKI once again poses in a karate stance)

NAGAINA: *(noticing audience)* Look at your friendssss, Rikki-tikki! They are funny looking and sssssmell delicioussssss! They are afraid. Better for me to eat them. *(she hisses and starts moving towards the audience)*

RIKKI-TIKKI: I'll destroy you just like I destroyed your husband Nag! Oh, and did I forget to tell you that I smashed all your eggs? 'Cause I totally did. Come fight me. You shall not be a widow long! *(NAGAINA stops and turns towards RIKKI-TIKKI)*

NAGAINA: You're dead, mongoossssse! *(she mimics RIKKI-TIKKI's karate pose; they fight but do not actually touch each other)*

RIKKI-TIKKI: Rikki-tikki-tch-tch! HI-YA! *(RIKKI-TIKKI karate chops NAGAINA and she dies melodramatically)*

BAGHEERA: *(doing a slow clap)* Bravo, Rikki-Tikki, bravo. But could you move along? What did I say earlier?

RIKKI-TIKKI: I know, I know, "It's not my play." Way to ruin the moment. *(to audience, sarcastically)* You're welcome! *(RIKKI-TIKKI drags NAGAINA offstage)*

(enter MOWGLI holding a pot)

MOWGLI: Got the fire...er, I mean, flower! *(winks to audience)*

BAGHEERA: Just in time...

(MOWGLI and BAGHEERA stay on stage)

(enter AKELA, TABAQUI, SHERE KHAN, FATHER WOLF, MOTHER WOLF, GRAY BROTHER, and WOLVES)

SHERE KHAN: Akela, your time as leader of the wolves is over.

TABAQUI: *(pulls up a chair and talks to the audience)* This should be interesting! Wish I had some popcorn.

FATHER WOLF: Akela has been an awesome leader, Shere Khan.

SHERE KHAN: Bah! What do we have to do with this toothless fool! He is doomed to die!

AKELA: Hey man, not cool! I'm not toothless.

SHERE KHAN: It is the man-cub who has lived too long. Free People, he was my meat from the first. Give him to me!

WOLVES: Yeah! He stinks too! Give him to the tiger!

AKELA: Chill out, guys. He is our brother in all but blood, and ye would kill him here! You're all cowards!

WOLVES: Boo! He is a man! *(pointing at MOWGLI)* Get lost, man-cub!

BAGHEERA: *(to MOWGLI)* I think now's the time...

MOWGLI: You keep saying that "I am a man", so I guess instead of brothers, I need to call you dogs. And guess what? Dogs are scared of fire, aren't they? *(MOWGLI runs around to the WOLVES, TABAQUI and SHERE KHAN and shakes the pot of fire in their faces. They all fling themselves to the ground in terror)*

SHERE KHAN: It burns! Oh how it burns!!

TABAQUI: My eyes!

MOWGLI: Serves you right! Now I will go to men. I'm done with the jungle. *(walks over to MOTHER WOLF, FATHER WOLF and GRAY BROTHER)* Ye will not forget me?

GRAY BROTHER: Never!

FATHER WOLF: Come soon! We be old, thy mother and I.

MOTHER WOLF: Come soon! I loved thee more than ever I loved my cubs.

GRAY BROTHER: *(sarcastically to MOTHER WOLF)* Hey, I'm standing right here!

MOWGLI: I'll come back once I've killed Shere Khan. Do not forget me! Tell them in the jungle never to forget me!

SHERE KHAN: *(to self)* I won't forget you Mowgli! *(does an evil, evil laugh!)* Muahahahahaha! ROAR!

(ALL exit)

ACT 2 SCENE 3

(enter MOWGLI and MESSUA with BULDEO from opposite side of the stage)

MOWGLI: *(pointing at audience)* Look, humans! *(calls out)* We be of one blood, ye and I! *(to audience)* Oh wait, you probably don't speak jungle, do you?

MESSUA: Look, Buldeo, a random wild boy!

BULDEO: Hmmm. Perhaps a wolf-child run away from the jungle? Hey, Messua, he looks like your son that was taken by the tiger a long time ago. The one with the weird name.

MESSUA: Holy cow! He does! *(to MOWGLI)* Nathoo! Nathoo!

MOWGLI: Bless you. By the way. I'm Mowgli.

MESSUA: Great! How did you learn how to speak?

MOWGLI: From a bear and a panther.

MESSUA: Oh...that's strange. Anyway, you're going to be my replacement son! *(she hugs him)*

MOWGLI: Hmmm, a bit weird, but, okay!

BULDEO: Welcome to our village, little wolf-dude.

(enter GRAY BROTHER)

GRAY BROTHER: Pssssssst! Hey, Mowgli!

MOWGLI: *(to MESSUA and BULDEO)* I'll be right back. *(runs to GRAY BROTHER)* Hey brother, what's up?

GRAY BROTHER: Just wanted to let you know that, *(sniffs and plugs nose)* phew, you smell gross! Where was I... oh yeah, Shere Khan still wants to kill you.

MOWGLI: Thanks for the warning. Let me know when he gets close. *(runs back to MESSUA and BULDEO; GRAY BROTHER exits)*

BULDEO: Okay, look. Everyone has a job here, even the kids. You can go watch the buffalo graze in the field. *(points at the audience implying they are the buffalo)* Cool?

MOWGLI: Cool.

MESSUA: Be safe, Nathoo...Mowgli...whatever your name is. Bye! *(MESSUA and BULDEO exit; MOWGLI sits down)*

MOWGLI: Watching buffalo is booooring.

(enter GRAY BROTHER AND AKELA)

GRAY BROTHER: Shere Khan is back, Mowgli! He's waiting for you in the ravine!

MOWGLI: *(jumps up)* Awesome. I am not afraid of Shere Khan. We have big work in hand. I have an idea, see all these buffalo? *(he gestures to the audience)*

AKELA: *(sarcastically)* Um, sure we do.

MOWGLI: We are going to drive these buffalo and trample Shere Khan to death!

AKELA: Sounds good. Very realistic.

MOWGLI: Watch, I will get them to practice stampeding *(demonstrates to audience to practice "stampeding" by stomping their feet down)*

MOWGLI: *(calls offstage)* Hey!! Shere Khan! Come out, come out wherever you are!

(enter SHERE KHAN)

SHERE KHAN: Who calls? *(gasps)* It's you. Finally, the time has come! Muahahahahaha! ROAR!

MOWGLI: *(to AKELA and GRAY BROTHER)* Go! *(MOWGLI, GRAY BROTHER and AKELA get the audience to start stampeding with their hands and feet in big motions.)*

SHERE KHAN: NOOOOO! Trampled to death by buffalo! *(to audience)* Very realistic! AGHHHHHHH!!! *(Shere Khan now falls to the ground and rolls around melodramatically, finally dying)*

MOWGLI: Ha ha! It is all over.

(enter BULDEO and MESSUA)

BULDEO: What is this folly! You didn't kill this tiger all by yourself, did you?

MOWGLI: No, they helped. *(he casually throws his arms around AKELA and GRAY BROTHER).* Nice work, friends! *(MOWGLI, AKELA and GRAY BROTHER high five each other and laugh together)*

BULDEO: Wait, you can talk to animals?! *(suddenly VERY scared)* Sorcerer! Wolf's brat! Jungle demon! Go away!

MOWGLI: Whoa! Now what is this? Did I do something wrong?

MESSUA: Oh, my son, go away or Buldeo will kill thee. Villagers are really scared of little boys who talk to animals. It was nice knowing you Nathoo...Mowgli... whatever your name is. Bye! *(MESSUA exits)*

MOWGLI: Fare you well, children of men! I'm outta here. *(to AKELA and GRAY BROTHER)* Come on guys, let's go back to the jungle.

(ALL exit)

ACT 2 SCENE 4

(enter MOWGLI, AKELA, GRAY BROTHER, FATHER WOLF, MOTHER WOLF, BAGHEERA, BALOO, and WOLVES)

MOWGLI: *(to MOTHER WOLF)* They have cast me out from the Man-Pack, but it's okay because we killed Shere Khan!

(SHERE KHAN enters and dies again; all the WOLVES give a big "hooray!")

MOTHER WOLF: Nice work, Little Frog.

FATHER WOLF: We're proud of you.

BAGHEERA: We were lonely in the jungle without thee.

MOWGLI: Aw, shucks. I missed you guys too.

BALOO: Gross, this is getting way too sappy.

WOLVES: Lead us again, O Akela. Lead us again, O Man-cub!

BAGHEERA: No way. Ye fought for freedom, and it is yours. Eat it, O Wolves.

MOWGLI: I think I like being free. I don't want to belong to any pack! Now I will hunt alone in the jungle.

ALL WOLVES: And we will hunt with thee.

MOWGLI: I said 'alone' didn't I? Oh well, it's good to have friends. I'm hungry...let's hunt!

ALL: HOWL!!!!!

(ALL exit running)

THE END

Sneak Peeks at other Playing With Plays books:

Two Gentlemen of Verona for Kids

ANTONIO: It's not nothing.

PROTEUS: Ahhhhh......It's a letter from Valentine, telling me what a great time he's having in Milan, yeah... that's what it says!

ANTONIO: Awesome! Glad to hear it! Because, you leave tomorrow to join Valentine in Milan.

PROTEUS: What!? Dad! No way! I don't want... I mean, I need some time. I've got some things to do.

ANTONIO: Like what?

PROTEUS: You know...things! Important things! And stuff! Lots of stuff!

ANTONIO: No more excuses! Go pack your bag. *(ANTONIO begins to exit)*

PROTEUS: Fie!

ANTONIO: What was that?

PROTEUS: Fiiii......ne with me, Pops! *(ANTONIO exits)* I was afraid to show my father Julia's letter, lest he should take exceptions to my love; and my own lie of an excuse made it easier for him to send me away.

ANTONIO: *(Offstage)* Proteus! Get a move on!!

PROTEUS: Fie!!!

(exit)

ACT 2 SCENE 1

(enter VALENTINE and SPEED following)

VALENTINE: Ah, Silvia, Silvia! *(heavy sighs)*

SPEED: *(mocking)* Madam Silvia! Madam Silvia! Gag me.

VALENTINE: Knock it off! You don't know her.

SPEED: Do too. She's the one that you can't stop staring at. Makes me wanna barf.

VALENTINE: I do not stare!

SPEED: You do. AND you keep singing that silly love song. *(sing INSERT SAPPY LOVE SONG)* You used to be so much fun.

VALENTINE: Huh? *(heavy sigh, starts humming SAME LOVE SONG)*

SPEED: Never mind.

VALENTINE: I have loved her ever since I saw her. Here she comes!

SPEED: Great. *(to audience)* Watch him turn into a fool.

(enter SILVIA)

VALENTINE: Hey, Silvia.

SILVIA: Hey, Valentine. What's goin' on?

VALENTINE: Nothin'. What's goin' on with you?

SILVIA: Nothin'.

(pause)

VALENTINE: What are you doing later?

SILVIA: Not sure. Prob-ly nothin'. You?

VALENTINE: Me neither. Nothin'.

SILVIA: Yea?

VALENTINE: Probably.

SPEED: *(to audience)* Kill me now.

SILVIA: Well, I guess I better go.

VALENTINE: Oh, okay! See ya'..

(pause)

SILVIA: See ya' later maybe?

VALENTINE: Oh, yea! Maybe! Yea! Okay!

SILVIA: Bye.

VALENTINE: Bye!

(exit SILVIA)

SPEED: *(aside)* Wow. *(to VALENTINE)* Dude, what the heck was that?

VALENTINE: I think she has a boyfriend. I can tell.

SPEED: Dude! She is so into you! How could you not see that?

VALENTINE: Do you think?

SPEED: Come on. We'll talk it through over dinner. *(to audience)* Fool. Am I right?

(exit)

Christmas Carol for Kids

(enter GHOST PRESENT wearing a robe and holding a turkey leg and a goblet)

GHOST PRESENT: Wake up, Scrooge! I am the Ghost of Christmas Present. Look upon me!

SCROOGE: I'm looking. Not that impressed. But let's get on with it.

GHOST PRESENT: Touch my robe! *(SCROOGE touches GHOST PRESENT's robe. Pause. They look at each other)* Er...it must be broken. Guess we walk. Come on. *(they begin walking downstage)*

SCROOGE: Where are we going?

GHOST PRESENT: Your employee, Bob Cratchit's house. Oh look, here we are.

(enter BOB, MRS. CRATCHIT, MARTHA CRATCHIT, and TINY TIM, who has a crutch in one hand; they are all holding bowls)

BOB: *(to audience)* Hi, we're the Cratchit family. We are a REALLY happy family!

MRS. CRATCHIT: *(to audience)* Yes, but we're REALLY poor, too. Thanks to HIS boss! *(pointing at BOB)*

MARTHA: *(to audience)* Yeah, as you can see our bowls are empty. *(shows empty bowl)* We practically survive off air.

TINY TIM: *(to audience)* But we're happy!

MRS. CRATCHIT: *(to audience; overly sappy)* Because we have each other.

TINY TIM: And love!

SCROOGE: *(to GHOST PRESENT)* Seriously, are they for real?

GHOST PRESENT: Yep! Adorable, isn't it?

BOB: A merry Christmas to us all.

TINY TIM: God bless us every one!

SCROOGE: Spirit, tell me if Tiny Tim will live.

GHOST PRESENT: *(puts hands to head as if looking into the future)* Ooooo, not so good...I see a vacant seat in the poor chimney corner, and a crutch without an owner. If SOMEBODY doesn't change SOMETHING, the child will die.

SCROOGE: No, no! Say he will be spared.

GHOST PRESENT: Nope, can't do that, sorry. Unless SOMEONE decides to change... hint, hint.

BOB: A Christmas toast to my boss, Mr. Scrooge! The founder of the feast!

MRS. CRATCHIT: *(angrily)* Oh sure, Mr. Scrooge! If he were here I'd give him a piece of my mind to feast upon. What an odious, stingy, hard, unfeeling man!

BOB: Dear, it's Christmas day. He's not THAT bad. *(Pause)* He's just... THAT sad. *(BOB holds up his bowl)* Come on, kids, to Scrooge! He probably needs it more than us!

MARTHA & TINY TIM: *(holding up their bowls)* To Scrooge!

MRS. CRATCHIT: *(muttering)* Thanks for nothing.

BOB: That's not nice.

MARTHA: And we Cratchits are ALWAYS nice. Read the book, Mom.

MRS. CRATCHIT: Sorry.

(the CRATCHIT FAMILY exits)

SCROOGE: She called me odious! Do I really smell that bad?

GHOST PRESENT: Odious doesn't mean you stink. Although in this case you do... According to the dictionary, odious means "unequivocally detestable." I mean, you are a toad sometimes Mr. Scrooge.

SCROOGE: Wow... that's kind of... mean.

The Tempest for Kids

PROSPERO: Hast thou, spirit, performed to point the tempest that I bade thee?

ARIEL: What? Was that English?

PROSPERO: *(Frustrated)* Did you make the storm hit the ship?

ARIEL: Why didn't you say that in the first place? Oh yeah! I rocked that ship! They didn't know what hit them.

PROSPERO: Why, that's my spirit! But are they, Ariel, safe?

ARIEL: Not a hair perished.

PROSPERO: Woo-hoo! All right. We've got more work to do.

ARIEL: Wait a minute. You're still going to free me, right, Master?

PROSPERO: Oh, I see. Is it sooooo terrible working for me? Huh? Remember when I saved you from that witch? Do you? Remember when that blue-eyed hag locked you up and left you for dead? Who saved you? Me, that's who!

ARIEL: I thank thee, master.

PROSPERO: I will free you in two days, okay? Sheesh. Patience is a virtue, or haven't you heard. Right. Where was I? Oh yeah... I need you to disguise yourself like a sea nymph and then... *(PROSPERO whispers something in ARIEL'S ear)* Got it?

ARIEL: Got it. *(ARIEL exits)*

PROSPERO: *(to MIRANDA)* Awake, dear heart, awake!

(MIRANDA yawns loudly)

PROSPERO: Shake it off. Come on. We'll visit Caliban, my slave.

MIRANDA: The witch's son? You mean the MONSTER! He's creepy and stinky!!!

PROSPERO: Mysterious and sneaky,

MIRANDA: Altogether freaky,

MIRANDA & PROSPERO: He's Caliban the slave!!! *(snap, snap!)*

PROSPERO: *(Calls offstage)* What, ho! Slave! Caliban!

(enter CALIBAN)

CALIBAN: Oh, look it's the island stealers! This is my home! My mother, the witch, left it to me and now you treat me like dirt.

MIRANDA: Oh boo-hoo! I used to feel sorry for you, I even taught you our language, but you tried to hurt me so now we have to lock you in that cave.

CALIBAN: I wish I had never learned your language!

PROSPERO: Go get us wood! If you don't, I'll rack thee with old cramps, and fill all thy bones with aches!

CALIBAN: *(to AUDIENCE)* He's so mean to me! But I have to do what he says. ANNOYING! *(exit CALIBAN)*

(enter FERDINAND led by "invisible" ARIEL)

ARIEL: *(Singing)* Who let the dogs out?! Woof, woof, woof!! *(Spookily)* The watchdogs bark; bow-wow, bow-wow!

FERDINAND: *(Dancing across stage)* Where should this music be? Where is it taking me! What's going on?

Hamlet for Kids

(enter GERTRUDE and POLONIUS)

GERTRUDE: What's up, Polonius?

POLONIUS: I am going to hide and spy on your conversation with Hamlet!

GERTRUDE: Oh, okay.

(POLONIUS hides somewhere, enter HAMLET very mad, swinging his sword around)

HAMLET: MOM!!! I AM VERY MAD!

GERTRUDE: Ahhh! You scared me!

(POLONIUS sneezes from hiding spot)

HAMLET: *(not seeing POLONIUS)* How now, a rat? Who's hiding? *(stabs POLONIUS)*

POLONIUS: O, I am slain! Ohhhh the pain! *(dies on stage)*

GERTRUDE: Oh me, what has thou done?

HAMLET: Oops, I thought that was Claudius. Hmph, oh well... as I was saying, I AM MAD you married uncle Claudius!

GERTRUDE: Oh that, yeah, sorry. *(in a motherly voice)* Now, you just killed Polonius, clean up this mess and go to your room!

HAMLET: Okay Mom.

(all exit, HAMLET drags POLONIUS' body offstage)

ACT 4 SCENES 1-3

(enter GERTRUDE and CLAUDIUS)

GERTRUDE: Ahhh, Dear?

CLAUDIUS: Yeah?

GERTRUDE: Ummmm, you would not believe what I have seen tonight! Polonius is dead.

CLAUDIUS: WHAT!?

GERTRUDE: Yeah, Hamlet was acting a little crazy, Polonius sneezed or something, then Hamlet yelled, "A rat, a rat!" and then WHACK! It was over.

CLAUDIUS: *(very angry)* HAMLET!!!! GET OVER HERE NOW!!!!!

(enter HAMLET)

CLAUDIUS: *(very casual)* Hey, what's up?

HAMLET: What noise, who calls on Hamlet? What do you want?

CLAUDIUS: Now, Hamlet. Where's Polonius' body?

HAMLET: I'm not telling!

CLAUDIUS: Oh come on, please tell me!!! Please! With a cherry on top! Where is Polonius?

HAMLET: Oh, all right. He's over there, up the stairs into the lobby. *(points offstage)*

(POLONIUS enters and dies again)

CLAUDIUS: Ewe... he's a mess! Hamlet, I am sending you off to England.

HAMLET: Fine! Farewell, dear Mother. And I'm taking this with me! *(HAMLET grabs POLONIUS and drags him offstage)*

(all exit but CLAUDIUS)

CLAUDIUS: *(to audience)* I have arranged his execution in England! *(laughs evilly as he exits)* Muwahahaha...

Sneak peek of
Taming of the Shrew for Kids

ACT 1 SCENE 1

(Enter LUCENTIO and TRANIO)

LUCENTIO: Well, Tranio, my trusty servant, here we are in Padua, Italy! I can't wait to start studying and learn all about philosophy and virtue!

TRANIO: There is such a thing as too much studying, master Lucentio. We need to remember to have fun too! PARTY!

LUCENTIO: Hey look! Here come some of the locals!

(LUCENTIO and TRANIO move to side of stage; Enter BAPTISTA, KATHERINA, BIANCA, HORTENSIO and GREMIO)

BAPTISTA: Look guys, you know the rules: Bianca can't marry anybody until her older sister, Katherina, is married. That's the plan and I'm sticking to it! If either of you both love Katherina, then please, take her.

KATHERINA: *(Sarcastically)* Wow, thanks Dad.

HORTENSIO: I wouldn't marry her if she were the last woman on earth.

KATHERINA: And I'd rather scratch your face off than marry you!

TRANIO: *(Aside to LUCENTIO)* That wench is stark mad!

BAPTISTA: Enough of this! Bianca, go inside.

BIANCA: Yes, dearest father. My books and

instruments shall be my company. *(She exits)*

KATHERINA: *(At BIANCA)* Goody two-shoes.

BAPTISTA: Bianca is so talented in music, instruments, and poetry! I really need to hire some tutors for her. *(KATHERINA rolls her eyes and sighs)* Good-day everyone! *(BAPTISTA exits)*

KATHERINA: *(Very angry)* AGHHHH!!!! I'm outta here

(Exits opposite direction from her father)

GREMIO: *(Shudders)* Ugh! How could anyone ever want to marry Katherina?!

HORTENSIO: I don't know, but let's find a husband for her.

GREMIO: A husband? A devil!

HORTENSIO: I say a husband.

GREMIO: I say a devil.

HORTENSIO: Alright, alright! There's got to be a guy out there crazy enough to marry her.

GREMIO: Let's get to it!

(Exit GREMIO and HORTENSIO)

LUCENTIO: Oh, Tranio! Sweet Bianca, has stolen my heart! I burn, I pine, I perish! Oh, how I love her!

TRANIO: Whoa, Master! You're getting a little over dramatic, there, Lucentio.

LUCENTIO: Sorry. But my heart is seriously on fire! How am I going to make her fall in love with me if she's not allowed to date anybody? Hmmm...

TRANIO: What if you pretended to be a tutor and went to teach her?

LUCENTIO: YOU ARE BRILLIANT, TRANIO! And because we're new here and no one knows what we look like yet, YOU will pretend to be ME at all the local parties. Quick, let's change clothes.

TRANIO: Here? Now?

LUCENTIO: Yes, Here and now! You can't stop this lovin' feeling! *(Starts singing a love song)*

TRANIO: Please, no singing. I'll do it. *(They exchange hats, socks or jackets)*

Sneak peek of
Oliver Twist
for Kids

(enter FAGIN, SIKES, DODGER and NANCY)

DODGER: So that Oliver kid got caught by the police.

FAGIN: He could tell them all our secrets and get us in trouble; we've got to find him. Like, in the next 30 seconds or so.

SIKES: Send Nancy. She's good at getting information quick.

NANCY: Nope. Don't wanna go, Sikes. I like the kid.

SIKES: She'll go, Fagin.

NANCY: No, she won't, Fagin.

SIKES: Yes, she will, Fagin.

NANCY: Fine! Grrrrr....

(NANCY sticks out her tongue at SIKES and storms offstage, then immediately returns)

NANCY: Okay, I checked with my sources and, some gentleman took him home to take care of him.

(NANCY, DODGER and SIKES stare at FAGIN waiting for direction)

FAGIN: Where?

NANCY: I don't know.

FAGIN: WHAT!?!? *(waiting)* Well don't just stand there, GO FIND HIM! *(to audience)* Can't find any good help these days!

(all run offstage, bumping into each other in their haste)

ACT 2 SCENE 2

(enter OLIVER)

OLIVER: *(to audience)* I'm out running an errand for Mr. Brownlow to prove that I'm a trustworthy boy. I can't keep hanging out with thieves, right?

(enter NANCY, who runs over to OLIVER and grabs him; SIKES, FAGIN, and DODGER enter shortly after and follow NANCY)

NANCY: Oh my dear brother! I've found him! Oh! Oliver! Oliver!

OLIVER: What!?!? I don't have a sister!

NANCY: You do now, kid. Let's go. *(she drags OLIVER to FAGIN)*

FAGIN: Dodger, take Oliver and lock him up.

DODGER: *(to OLIVER)* Sorry, dude. *(DODGER and OLIVER start to exit)*

OLIVER: Aw, man! Seriously? I just found a good home...

NANCY: Don't be too mean to him, Fagin.

OLIVER: *(as he's exiting)* Yeah, don't be too mean to me, Fagin!

SIKES: *(mimicking NANCY)* Don't be mean, Fagin. Wah, wah, wah. Look, I need Oliver to help me rob a house, okay? He is just the size I want to fit through the window. All sneaky ninja like.

Much Ado About Nothing
for Kids

ACT 1 SCENE 1

(Enter LEONATO, HERO, and BEATRICE)

LEONATO: *(to audience)* I am The Governor. Governor of Messina, Italy.

HERO: Whatever, Dad. You are always talking about yourself. We know you're "The Governor". We've got it. *(sarcastically)* Governor Leonato.

LEONATO: Now listen to me, Hero. You need to behave yourself. We have guests coming. *(BEATRICE laughs at Hero)* And you Beatrice, you better watch your tongue, because I don't want you getting into a "war of words" with Benedick, again. Got me? Look, here comes a messenger.

(enter MESSENGER)

MESSENGER: Sir, I come to tell you that Don Pedro, the Prince of Arragon, his brother Don John, and his faithful men, Claudio and Benedick, will all be coming soon.

(exit MESSENGER)

HERO: Oh, goodie! I think Claudio is cute!

BEATRICE: Yeah, well, Benedick is NOT! He's always smelly after a battle! Oh look, here comes the smelly one now.

(enter DON JOHN, DON PEDRO, BENEDICK, and CLAUDIO)

LEONATO: Welcome, Don Pedro and friends! You have fought bravely. Please stay and party with us.

DON PEDRO: We will, thank you!

DON JOHN: *(aside and pouting to the audience)* My brother gets all the attention! I hate him!

DON PEDRO: Don John, what are you saying over there?

DON JOHN: Oh nothing, dear brother. *(starts dancing VERY badly)* Just practicing my dance moves for the party!

BEATRICE: *(mockingly to BENEDICK)* So Benedick, you're back again? *(sniffs him)* And, whew! *(plugging her nose with her fingers)* Smelly as usual.

BENEDICK: *(mockingly in a high girl's voice)* "Smelly as usual" You, my dear Beatrice, are a pain as usual. Are you ready to continue our merry war?

BEATRICE: You mean our war of words? You know it!

BENEDICK: You are such a parrot-teacher.

BEATRICE: What did you call me?

BENEDICK: Someone who talks A LOT! What's the matter? Forget your dictionary? You know, *(said slowly as if she doesn't understand English)* PARROT TEACHER.

BEATRICE: Humph! A bird of my tongue is better than a beast of yours!

BENEDICK: I wish my horse had the speed of your tongue!

BEATRICE: *(to audience)* Oh, he makes me sooooo mad! *(BEATRICE stomps her feet like a 4-year old and storms offstage)*

LEONATO: *(to audience)* There's a skirmish of wit between them. *(to all)* Everyone, let's go to my castle.

You know, the castle that belongs to The Governor? *(with two thumbs pointing at himself)*

(all exit except CLAUDIO and BENEDICK)

CLAUDIO: *(to BENEDICK)* Hero is sooooooo cute!

BENEDICK: Whoa, did you just say, "cute"? No, no, no, NO! A kitten is cute, a baby is cute, but her? No. With a name like "Hero", she can NOT be cute!

CLAUDIO: Yeah, what about her name?

BENEDICK: Come on. "Hero?" Does she drive the Batmobile and wear a cape, too?

CLAUDIO: Leave her alone because...because...because I think I want to marry her!

BENEDICK: Marry? Whoa, buddy! Listen, I mean, she's a bit..... plain. Actually, I do not like her. And as for marriage, it's overrated, so last year. You'll never catch me getting married. That's right, the single life for me!

CLAUDIO: *(CLAUDIO is day dreamy and lovesick)* She is the sweetest lady that I ever looked on. Could you buy such a jewel?

BENEDICK: *(to audience)* And a case to put her into.

(enter DON PEDRO)

DON PEDRO: Where have you guys been?

BENEDICK: You won't believe this! Lovesick Claudio here wants to marry Hero. Hah! Isn't that hilarious!?

DON PEDRO: Be careful Benedick, my friend. Remember, this is a comedy, and all of Shakespeare's comedies end in marriage.

CLAUDIO: Yeah!

The Three Musketeers
for Kids

(ATHOS and D'ARTAGNAN enter)

ATHOS: Glad you could make it. I have engaged two of my friends as seconds.

D'ARTAGNAN: Seconds?

ATHOS: Yeah, they make sure we fight fair. Oh, here they are now!

(enter ARAMIS and PORTHOS singing, "Bad boys, bad boys, watcha gonna do...")

PORTHOS: Hey! I'm fighting him in an hour. I am going to fight... because...well... I am going to fight!

ARAMIS: And I fight him at two o'clock! Ours is a theological quarrel. *(does a thinking pose)*

D'ARTAGNAN: Yeah, yeah, yeah... I'll get to you soon!

ATHOS: We are the Three Musketeers; Athos, Porthos, and Aramis.

D'ARTAGNAN: Whatever, Ethos, Pathos, and Logos, let's just finish this! *(swords crossed and are about to fight; enter JUSSAC and cardinal's guards)*

PORTHOS: The cardinal's guards! Sheathe your swords, gentlemen.

JUSSAC: Dueling is illegal! You are under arrest!

ARAMIS: *(to ATHOS and PORTHOS)* There are five of them and we are but three.

D'ARTAGNAN: *(steps forward to join them)* It appears to me we are four! I have the spirit; my heart is that of a Musketeer.

PORTHOS: Great! I love fighting!

(Musketeers say "Fight, fight fight!...Fight, fight, fight!" as they are fighting; D'ARTAGNAN fights JUSSAC and it's the big fight; JUSSAC is wounded and exits; the 3 MUSKETEERS cheer)

ATHOS: Well done! Let's go see Treville and the king!

ARAMIS: And we don't have to kill you now!

PORTHOS: And let's get some food, too! I'm hungry!

D'ARTAGNAN: *(to audience)* This is fun!

(ALL exit)

ACT 2 SCENE 1

(enter 3 MUSKETEERS, D'ARTAGNAN, and TREVILLE)

TREVILLE: The king wants to see you, and he's not too happy you killed a few of the cardinal's guards.

(enter KING)

KING: *(yelling)* YOU GUYS HUMILIATED THE CARDINAL'S GUARDS!

ATHOS: Sire, they attacked us!

KING: Oh...Well then, bravo! I hear D'Artagnan beat the cardinal's best swordsman! Brave young man! Here's some money for you. Enjoy! *(hands money to D'ARTAGNAN)*

D'ARTAGNAN: Sweet!

(ALL exit)

Sneak peek of
Henry V for Kids

ACT 2 SCENE 2

(enter BEDFORD and EXETER, observing CAMBRIDGE and SCROOP, who whisper among themselves)

BEDFORD: Hey Exeter, do you think it's a good idea that King Henry is letting those conspirators wander around freely?

EXETER: It's alright, Bedford. King Henry has a plan! He knows EVERYTHING they are plotting. BUT, they don't KNOW he knows. And HE knows that they don't know he knows...and...

BEDFORD: *(interrupting)* Okay, okay, I get it. Let's go sit in the audience and watch! *(they sit in the audience; enter HENRY)*

HENRY: Greetings, my good and FAITHFUL friends, Cambridge and Scroop. Perfect timing! I need your advice on something.

CAMBRIDGE: Sure thing. You know we'd do anything for you! Never was a monarch better feared and loved.

SCROOP: That's why we're going to kick some French butt!! *(SCROOP and CAMBRIDGE high-five)*

HENRY: Excellent! A man was arrested yesterday for shouting nasty things about me. But I'm sure by now he's thought better of it. I think I ought to show mercy and pardon him.

SCROOP: Nah, let him be punished.

HENRY: Ahhh, but let us yet be merciful.

CAMBRIDGE: Nah, I'm with Scroop! Off with his head!

HENRY: Is that your final answer?

CAMBRIDGE & SCROOP: YES!

HENRY: Ok, but if we don't show mercy for small offenses, how will we show mercy for big ones? I will release him. Now, take a look at THESE LETTERS.

(as CAMBRIDGE and SCROOP read the letters, their jaws drop)

HENRY: Why, how now, gentlemen? What see you in those papers that your jaws hang so low?

EXETER: *(to audience)* The letters betray their guilt!

CAMBRIDGE: I do confess my fault...

SCROOP:...and do submit me to your Highness' mercy! *(they start begging and pleading on the ground)*

HENRY: Exeter, Bedford, arrest these traitors. What did they say... Oh yeah, OFF WITH THEIR HEADS!

CAMBRIDGE: Whoa there!

SCROOP: Off with our what? What happened to the whole "mercy" thing you were just talking about!?

HENRY: Your own words talked me out of it! Take them away!

CAMBRIDGE: Well, this stinks!

(EXETER and BEDFORD arrest CAMBRIDGE and SCROOP; ALL exit, except HENRY)

HENRY: Being king is no fun sometimes. Scroop used to be one of my best friends. *(SCROOP runs on stage and dies melodramatically)* But there's no time to mope! *(CAMBRIDGE runs on stage and dies on top of SCROOP)* The signs of war advance. No king of England, if not King of France! NOW CLEAN UP THIS MESS!

(EXETER and BEDFORD run on stage and drag bodies off; exit HENRY)

Richard III for Kids

ACT 1 SCENE 4

(CLARENCE is in prison, sleeping. He wakes up from a bad dream)

CLARENCE: Terrible, horrible, no good, very bad dream! *(pauses, notices audience and addresses them)* O, I have pass'd a miserable night! I dreamt that Richard was trying to kill me! Hahahaha, Richard is SUCH a good guy, he would NEVER do a thing like that!

(enter MURDERER carrying a weapon)

MURDERER: I sounded like such a pro, no one will know it's my first day on the job! Hehehe!

CLARENCE: Hey! Who's there?

MURDERER: Um... um... *(hides his murder weapon behind his back)*

CLARENCE: Your eyes do menace me. Are you planning to murder me? 'Cause that's not a good idea. My brother Richard is a REALLY powerful guy.

MURDERER: Ha! Richard is the one who sent me here to do this! *(a pause)* Whoops...

CLARENCE: Hahaha, you foolish fellow. Richard loves me.

MURDERER: Dude, what are you not getting? He PAID me to do this!

CLARENCE: O, do not slander him, for he is kind.

(The MURDERER stabs CLARENCE. CLARENCE dies a dramatic death)

CLARENCE: Kinda ruthless... *(dies)*

MURDERER: *(Gasps)* Oh, my! He's dead! I feel bad now... I bet Clarence was a really nice guy. Ahhh, the guilt! Wow, I should have stayed in clown school.

(MURDERER exits)

ACT 2 SCENE 1

(KING EDWARD is surrounded by QUEEN ELIZABETH and BUCKINGHAM)

KING EDWARD: Well, this has been a great day at work! Everyone's agreed to get along!

(ELIZABETH and BUCKINGHAM shake hands with each other to celebrate the peace. Enter RICHARD. KING EDWARD smiles happily)

KING EDWARD: If I die, I will be at peace! But I must say I'm feeling a lot healthier after all of this peace-making!

RICHARD: Hey! Looks like you're all in a good mood. That's great, 'cause you know I LOVE getting along! So what's up?

KING EDWARD: I made them like each other!

RICHARD: How lovely! I like you all now, too! Group hug? *(everyone shakes their head)* No? *(he grins sweetly)*

ELIZABETH: Wonderful! Once Clarence gets back from the Tower, everything will be perfect!

RICHARD: WHAT??? We make peace and then you insult us like this? That's no way to talk about a DEAD man!!

(EVERYONE gasps)

KING EDWARD: Is Clarence dead? I told them to cancel the execution!

RICHARD: Oh, yeah... guess that was too late! *(winks to audience)*

KING EDWARD: Nooooooo!!!! Oh my poor brother! Now I feel more sick than EVER! Oh, poor Clarence!

(All exit except RICHARD and BUCKINGHAM)

RICHARD: Well, that sure worked as planned!

BUCKINGHAM: Great job, partner!

(both exit, laughing evilly)

Treasure Island
for Kids

(enter JIM, TRELAWNEY, and DOCTOR; enter CAPTAIN SMOLLETT from the other side of the stage)

TRELAWNEY: Hello Captain. Are we all shipshape and seaworthy?

CAPTAIN: Trelawney, I don't know what you're thinking, but I don't like this cruise; and I don't like the men.

TRELAWNEY: *(very angry)* Perhaps you don't like the ship?

CAPTAIN: Nope, I said it short and sweet.

DOCTOR: What? Why?

CAPTAIN: Because I heard we are going on a treasure hunt and the coordinates of the island are: *(whispers to DOCTOR)*

DOCTOR: Wow! That's exactly right!

CAPTAIN: There's been too much blabbing already.

DOCTOR: Right! But, I doubt ANYTHING will go wrong!

CAPTAIN: Fine. Let's sail!

(ALL exit)

Act 2 Scene 3

(enter JIM, SILVER, and various other pirates)

SILVER: Ay, ay, mates. You know the song: Fifteen men on the dead man's chest.

ALL PIRATES: Yo-ho-ho and a bottle of rum!

(PIRATES slowly exit)

JIM: *(to the audience)* So, the Hispaniola had begun her voyage to the Isle of Treasure. As for Long John, well, he still is the nicest cook...

SILVER: Do you want a sandwich?

JIM: That would be great, thanks Long John! *(SILVER exits; JIM addresses audience)* As you can see, Long John is a swell guy! Until...

(JIM hides in the corner)

Act 2 Scene 4

(enter SILVER and OTHER PIRATES)

JIM: *(to audience)* I overheard Long John talking to the rest of the pirates.

SILVER: Listen here you, Scallywags! I was with Captain Flint when he hid this treasure. And those cowards have the map. Follow my directions, and no killing, yet. Clear?

DICK: Clear.

SILVER: But, when we do kill them, I claim Trelawney. And remember, dead men don't bite.

GEORGE: Ay, ay, Long John!

(ALL exit but JIM)

JIM: *(to audience)* Oh no! Long John Silver IS the one-legged man that Billy Bones warned me about! I have to tell the others!

(JIM runs offstage)

King Lear for Kids

ACT 1 SCENE 1

KING LEAR's palace

(enter FOOL entertaining the audience with jokes, dancing, juggling, Hula Hooping... whatever the actor's skill may be; enter KENT)

KENT: Hey, Fool!

FOOL: What did you call me?!

KENT: I called you Fool.

FOOL: That's my name, don't wear it out! *(to audience)* Seriously, that's my name in the play!

(enter LEAR, CORNWALL, ALBANY, GONERIL, REGAN, and CORDELIA)

LEAR: The lords of France and Burgundy are outside. They both want to marry you, Cordelia.

ALL: Ooooooo!

LEAR: *(to audience)* Between you and me she IS my favorite child! *(to the girls)* Daughters, I need to talk to you about something. It's a really big deal.

GONERIL & REGAN: Did you buy us presents?

LEAR: This is even better than presents!

GONERIL & REGAN: Goody, goody!!!

CORDELIA: Father, your love is enough for me.

LEAR: Give me the map there, Kent. Girls, I'm tired. I've made a decision: Know that we - and by 'we' I mean 'me' - have divided in three our kingdom...

KENT: Whoa! Sir, dividing the kingdom may cause

chaos! People could die!

FOOL: Well, this IS a tragedy...

LEAR: You worry too much, Kent. I'm giving it to my daughters so their husbands can be rich and powerful... like me!

CORNWALL & ALBANY: Sweet!

GONERIL & REGAN: Wait... what?

CORDELIA: This is olden times. That means that everything we own belongs to our husbands.

GONERIL & REGAN: Olden times stink!

CORDELIA: Truth.

LEAR: So, my daughters, tell your daddy how much you love him. Goneril, our eldest-born, speak first.

GONERIL: Sir, I love you more than words can say! More than outer space, puppies and cotton candy! I love you more than any child has ever loved a father in the history of the entire world, dearest Pops!

CORDELIA: *(to audience)* Holy moly! Surely, he won't be fooled by that. *(to self)* Love, and be silent.

LEAR: Thanks, sweetie! I'm giving you this big chunk of the kingdom here. What says our second daughter, Our dearest Regan, wife to Cornwall? Speak.

REGAN: What she said, Daddy... times a thousand!

CORDELIA: *(to audience)* What?! I love my father more than either of them. But I can't express it in words. My love's more richer than my tongue.

LEAR: Wow, Regan! You get this big hunk of the kingdom. Cordelia, what can you tell me to get this giant piece of kingdom as your own? Speak.

CORDELIA: Nothing, my lord.

LEAR: Nothing?!?

CORDELIA: Nothing.

LEAR: Come on, now. Nothing will come of nothing.

CORDELIA: I love you as a daughter loves her father.

LEAR: Try a little, harder, sweetie!

CORDELIA: Why are my sisters married if they give you all their love?

LEAR: How did you get so mean?

CORDELIA: Father, I will not insult you by telling you my love is like... as big as a whale.

LEAR: *(getting mad)* Fine. I'll split your share between your sisters.

REGAN, GONERIL, & CORNWALL: Yessss!

KENT: Whoa! Let's all just calm down a minute!

LEAR: Peace, Kent! You don't want to mess with me right now. I told you she was my favorite...

GONERIL & REGAN: What!?

LEAR: ...and she can't even tell me she loves me more than a whale? Nope. Now I'm mad.

KENT: Royal Lear, really...

LEAR: Kent, I'm pretty emotional right now! You better not try to talk me out of this...

KENT: Sir, you're acting ... insane.

ABOUT THE AUTHORS

KHARA C. BARNHART first fell in love with Shakespeare in 8th grade after reading Hamlet, and she has been an avid fan ever since. She studied Shakespeare's works in Stratford-upon-Avon, and graduated with a degree in English from UCLA. Khara is lucky to have a terrific career and a charmed life on the Central Coast of CA, but what she cherishes most is time spent with her husband and children. She is delighted to have this chance to help kids foster their own appreciation of Shakespeare in a way that is educational, entertaining, and most importantly, fun!

BRENDAN P. KELSO came to writing modified Shakespeare scripts when he was taking time off from work to be at home with his newly born son. "It just grew from there". Within months, he was being asked to offer classes in various locations and acting organizations along the Central Coast of California. Originally employed as an engineer, Brendan never thought about writing. However, his unique personality, humor, and love for engaging the kids with The Bard has led him to leave the engineering world and pursue writing as a new adventure in life! He has always believed, "the best way to learn is to have fun!" Brendan makes his home on the Central Coast of California and loves to spend time with his wife and son.

CAST AUTOGRAPHS

Printed in Great Britain
by Amazon

63668161R00061